WHAT DOES
IT MEAN TO BE
POST-SOVIET?

ON DECOLONIALITY A SERIES EDITED BY
WALTER D. MIGNOLO AND CATHERINE E. WALSH

WHAT DOES IT MEAN TO BE POST-SOVIET?

DECOLONIAL ART FROM THE RUINS OF THE SOVIET EMPIRE

Madina Tlostanova

Duke University Press   Durham and London   2018

Text designed by Courtney Leigh Baker
Cover designed by Julienne Alexander
Typeset in Whitman and Trade Gothic by Westchester Publishing
Services

Library of Congress Cataloging-in-Publication Data
Names: Tlostanova, M. V. (Madina Vladimirovna), author.
Title: What does it mean to be post-Soviet? : decolonial art from the
ruins of the Soviet empire / Madina Tlostanova.
Description: Durham : Duke University Press, 2018. | Series:
On decoloniality | Includes bibliographical references and index.
Identifiers: LCCN 2017054363 (print) | LCCN 2017056841 (ebook)
ISBN 9780822371632 (ebook)
ISBN 9780822371342 (hardcover : alk. paper)
ISBN 9780822371274 (pbk. : alk. paper)
Subjects: LCSH: Postcolonialism and the arts—Former Soviet
republics. | Post-communism—Social aspects—Former Soviet
republics. | Art—Political aspects—Former Soviet republics.
Classification: LCC NX180.P67 (ebook) | LCC NX180.P67 T56
2018 (print) | DDC 700/.4—dc23
LC record available at https://lccn.loc.gov/2017054363

Cover art: Egor Rogalev, *Situation No. 7*. Kiev, 2009. Archival
photographic print in various editions; dimensions variable.
From the photo series *Synchronicity*. Courtesy of the artist.

CONTENTS

Acknowledgments vii

INTRODUCTION   A Futureless Ontology? 1

CHAPTER ONE   The Decolonial Sublime 25

CHAPTER TWO   Decolonial Aesthesis
                    and Post-Soviet Art 33

CHAPTER THREE   A Woman Who Has Many Selves
                    and Takes Over Many Spaces:
                    A Conversation with Liina Siib 65

CHAPTER FOUR   Beyond Dependencies: A Talk with
                    Vyacheslav Akhunov, the Lonely Ranger
                    of Uzbek Contemporary Art 84

CHAPTER FIVE   Reflecting on Time, Space, and Memory
                    with Afanassy Mamedov 105

CONCLUSION   People Are Silent . . . 119

                    Notes 129
                    References 135
                    Index 141

I warmly thank Catherine Walsh and Walter Mignolo, the coeditors of this important and timely book series at Duke University Press, for inviting me to publish one of its first volumes. I also thank Walter Mignolo, Pedro Pablo Gómez, and Rolando Vázquez for inviting me to write a series of articles on decolonial aesthesis in their edited collections and journals, including *Calle 14*, *Estéticas y opción decolonial*, *Arte y estética en la encrucijada descolonial*, and *Social Text Periscope*, and for giving me a chance to share my ideas and intuitions on the artistic and existential manifestations of the imperial difference at the annual Decolonial Summer Schools "Stolen Memories: Museums, Slavery and (De)coloniality" (2015) and "What Does It Mean to 'Decolonize'? Introducing the Decolonial Option" (2016) in Middelburg, the Netherlands.

I also cordially thank Sabine Broeck from the University of Bremen for inviting me to participate in a number of important conferences and seminars on decoloniality and postcolonial critique, among them the edited collection with Carsten Junker, *Postcoloniality—Decoloniality—Black Critique: Joints and Fissures* (2014), which allowed me to formulate some of the issues addressed in this book.

I thank the colleagues from Estonia, Latvia, Poland, Romania, and Slovakia with whom I have collaborated on different book and journal projects and conferences on the intersections of the post-socialist and postcolonial experience. Our discussions and debates were very helpful for the gestation of this book. In particular, I thank Dorota Kołodziejczyk, who invited me to participate in the "On Colonialism, Communism and East-Central Europe: Some Reflections" special issue of the *Journal of Postcolonial Writing*, which she coedited with Cristina Sandru. I express my gratitude to Dobrota Pucherová and Róbert Gáfric for inviting me to give a keynote speech at their conference "Postcolonialism and East-Central European Literatures" in Bratislava, Slovakia, in 2014 and for including my article in their collection *Postcolonial Europe? Essays on Post-Communist Literatures and Cultures* (2015). Another important venue for developing my views on the external imperial difference was an invited publication in *Intersections: East European Journal of Society and Politics* in Budapest. I am very grateful to its editor, Margit Feischmidt, for giving me this wonderful opportunity for exploring my ideas in international contexts and for developing the critique of the imperial difference.

I am grateful to my gender studies and Baltic studies colleagues from two Swedish universities—Linköping University and Södertorn University. In the last several years the Center for Baltic and East European Studies (CBEES) at Södertorn University and the Gender Studies Unit at Linköping University invited me several times as scholar-in-residence, visiting scholar, and keynote speaker. This has also allowed me to present my ongoing investigations in preparation for this book.

I thank several museums, galleries, curators, and art theorists for their generous invitations to participate in the educational and theoretical programs of several exhibitions, contemporary art biennials, and other related events, including Manifesta 10; the theoretical program of the Moscow Center of Contemporary Art; the Jewish Museum and Tolerance Center in Moscow; the Moscow Biennale of Contemporary Art; the Aspan Gallery in Almaty, Kazakhstan; the Media Impact Festival; Viktor Misiano's multiple projects on post-socialist artists and imaginaries and, particularly, his invitations to publish several texts in *Moscow Art Magazine*. This experience was invaluable for working on this book.

I am also grateful to the two anonymous readers of the first draft of this book. Their constructive and well-meaning suggestions and comments helped improve the manuscript.

Last but not least, I thank artists, writers and activists for their immensely important reflections that they shared with me in our interviews and personal dialogues. Among them, I am especially grateful to Vyacheslav Akhunov, Aslan Gaisumov, Taus Makhacheva, Afanassy Mamedov, Anton Nikolayev, Egor Rogalev, Liina Siib, and Saule Suleimenova.

Ultimately, in the war between the refrigerator (rising food prices) and the television set (the war in Ukraine), the refrigerator is likely to win.
—*The Economist*, December 17, 2014

INTRODUCTION

A Futureless Ontology?

I was writing this introduction at a very complex and rapidly changing global geopolitical moment when the very future existence of Russia as a separate state was becoming problematic. I was writing from the relatively safe position of chaired professor at a Swedish university, but I was and will always remain a product of the Russian and Soviet imperial legacies—a postcolonial other with ancestors originating in the Russian Orient and the Russian South—the two darker colonial spaces that are seldom taken into account in any imperial-colonial discussions. Therefore, I am a person from the darker side of the Russian/Soviet modernity/coloniality. In this book I focus mainly on the experiences, sensibilities and creative work of the postcolonial artists who happen to be at the same time postsoviet. Yet I would like to start with a few preliminary remarks on the evolution of the Russian imperial difference that, in tandem with the failed yet never buried Soviet modernity project, has led to today's stagnation, anomie, and looming disintegration.

The Imperial Difference Once Again

In several works coauthored with Walter Mignolo and in my own texts I have touched upon the specific nature of external imperial difference and Russia as a graphic example of such a difference (Tlostanova 2007, 2014, 2015; Tlostanova and Mignolo 2012).[1] To put it simply, starting from about the sixteenth century a global imperial hierarchy appeared in the emerging world system. Within this hierarchy several imperial leagues were formed and transformed in the course of time. In the post-Enlightenment modernity Spain, Italy, and Portugal moved to the position of the South of Europe and hence to the *internal* imperial difference that never collapsed into absolute or insurmountable forms. The Ottoman sultanate and Russia, on the contrary, became the zones of *the external* imperial difference, as they were rooted in different (from the core European norm) religions, languages, economic models, and ethnic-racial classifications. Both internal *and* external imperial others were never allowed to join the first league and become equal to Great Britain, France, or the United States today.

One might think that these markers ceased to be valid anymore. Yet in reality they continue to flourish and affect the global geopolitical relations, classifying people and defining the validity of their lives in line with the original matrix of modernity and its rigid human taxonomies and hierarchies. A terrorist act in Paris is unconditionally regarded, and represented, as a tragedy in both global mass media and social media, whereas the deaths of thousands of civilians daily in the Middle East go practically unnoticed. A quiet decay of Russia as the largest remnant of the Soviet empire would also remain completely uninteresting to the world which is indifferent to the fate of several dozen million people who have all become hostages of the inhumane regime. It is only the looming global nuclear threat and the neo-imperial geopolitical ambitions of the Russian administration, which is trying once again to break into the first league previously irremediably losing in its imperial status, which still keep Russia on the front pages. The pragmatic security discourses then remain the only justification for the rest of the world to continue paying attention to this faraway region pushed more and more out of the world system, and reduced in its rank from the semi-periphery to an ultimately peripheral status.

What is at work here can be called a rule of regressive turning of imperial difference into a colonial one, when a second-rate empire, in the imaginaries of the winning rivals, is regarded as a colony, soon starts to realize this status, and react in aggressive and negativist ways. Thus the failed Soviet modernity shifted into the colonial realm in relation to the winning neoliberal modernity/coloniality, yet retained some traces of its own, internal imperial-colonial structures and hierarchies, the most obvious of which is the colonizing attitude to the non-Western, postcolonial, post-Soviet others. But the very realization of this difference by the imperial ideologues allowed them to use this argument in their favor. And the Russian imperial revivalism acquired an opportunity to take the forms which externally resembled anticolonial struggles, at times appropriating the decolonial arguments, and trying on the role of the victim in global geopolitics. This is what is now taking place in Russia in its efforts to pretend to be a postcolonial subaltern and thus justify its revived imperial expansionism. But the wolf's fangs stick out of its sheep's clothing.

The Russian imperial difference triggers its specific schizophrenia, which is different from the classical Duboisean double-consciousness (Du Bois 1903) in its clearly negative stance. The imperial double-consciousness in contrast with the colonial one is unable to mutate into anything constructive; it either has to go or it has to be radically transformed into a different model. Russia is choking on its own rejection and fury addressed to both the stronger imperial rivals and the weaker colonial others.

Imperial difference in itself is evidence of the agonistic and rigidly hierarchical nature of modernity/coloniality. At its core is an implied and delocalized reference point that originally lay in the heart of Europe but has now shifted toward the Anglo-Saxon world, with its heart in the United States. The rest of the people are taxonomized along the human scale of modernity in relation to their proximity to this vantage point. Some are assigned a status of the forever catching-up agents or even voluntarily define it as their goal. Others are placed into the ghetto of absolute otherness and are withdrawn from history and modernity. As for the post-Soviet, and wider post-socialist, condition, in the past twenty-five years it has demonstrated the growing dispersal tendencies which remap the former Socialist subjects and position them along different vectors and within different alliances in the new world order where the precarious Socialist semi-periphery is rapidly sliding into a more and more chronic peripheral condition.

The post-Soviet trajectory of Russia and a number of its former colonies shows that they were first lured by the carrot of the catching-up modernization and even, in the case of the European semiperiphery, by the promise of getting back to the European bosom, but these models were grounded in false evolutionism. With different speeds and to different extents of realization of their failure most of these societies grasped that they would never be allowed or able to step from the darker side of modernity to the lighter one, from otherness to sameness. The only move they could count on is comprised of the small steps along the endless ladder of modernity that ultimately led nowhere yet always enchanted with a desired but unattainable horizon. A number of postsocialist communities started cultivating bitter reactions of disappointment in the European, and wider Western, project, and their critiques resembled, and even openly borrowed from, postcolonial arguments (Lazarus 2012; Slapšak 2012).

The East European countries were interpreted within the global neoliberal modernity/coloniality in a progressivist rather than Orientalist manner: they were considered to be reformable and eventually subject to European assimilation, yet always with an indelible difference. The postsocialist people were offered to accept, without question, the existing global hierarchy in which everyone is assigned a precise, fixed and never questioned place, and is afraid of losing that precarious position by being associated with countries—such as those of the global South—that stand even lower. The postsocialist countries' almost unanimous refusal to accept refugees, a position supported by both their governments and their populations and often verbalized in exclusionary, racist forms, should be interpreted not only through a simple economic rationale and the specific mythology of Eastern Europe acting as a sacrifice to inhuman communist regimes, but also, and more importantly, be interpreted as a trace of the modern/colonial rivalry that, in the case of these "new" Europeans, is not alleviated by discourses of welfare, charity, or solidarity.

Postcolonial Rhetoric Borrowed by Post-Socialist Countries

The appropriation of postcolonial and, at times, decolonial rhetoric in relation to the postsocialist countries in the increasingly unipolar (in despite of all the proclamations of multipolarity) world, has gone quite unevenly. In postsocialist Eastern Europe it was faster, more successful, and less censored because the liberating rhetoric logically shifted from the old dependence on Russia and the USSR to a critique of the new dependence on Western Europe and the United States without touching the interests of the new national elites. The discourse of postcolonialism was not only harmless, therefore; but was even somewhat useful for the newly independent states. The postsocialist intellectuals started to write about the subalternization and peripheralization of Eastern Europe and Central Europe and on the sensibility of European poor relatives who were forced from their real socialism into the real neoliberal capitalism, with no hope for success or, sometimes, even for mere survival (Kołodziejczyk and Sandru 2012; Pucherová and Gáfric 2015). Postsocialist artists such as Ciprian Mureşan and Tanja Ostojić have addressed the metaphors and imagery that intersect with postcolonial sensibilities, often through projecting these artistic means onto the contemporary global coloniality.

However, these sentiments did not lead to any wide-scale state Socialist renaissance movements, or even to simple nostalgia for the bygone Socialist days. One of the reasons is that in the Socialist system, these societies were already aware of their colonial status and humiliation due to the Soviet occupation. Being oppressed and then nostalgic about an earlier, albeit different form of, oppression would indeed be strange. The schism in relation to the West and efforts to merge with it in any function once again followed old, imperial borders. An interesting example is Ukraine, which was divided in its political preferences not only in accordance with the Russian population distribution during the Soviet years, but also along the older Austro-Hungarian borders with Russia. The Baltic countries provide another complex example: although they are unhappy about the harsh economic problems they now face and about the mass-migration of their populations to Western Europe, they are reluctant to revise their attitude that the Soviet occupation caused all of the problems. The Baltic littoral continues to see Germany and the Scandinavian countries as an El Dorado for the Baltic postsocialist migrants, even if their motherlands historically have had quite a painful and complex predicament of internal European colonization initiated by these same Western European role models (Kalnačs 2016a).

The situation of the non-European post-Soviet former colonies—in Central Asia and in the southern Caucasus (with the significant exception of Georgia)—is much different. Here the postcolonial and decolonial discourses of any political kind are tabooed, because the symbolic power and influence of the failed Soviet empire remained quite significant there until very recently. Therefore, any critique of Russian and Soviet expansionism is banned. In many cases it has also continued until now. Sympathies have often stayed on the Russian side and lingered in the mutual past, even if this past was highly mythologized and invented. In many cases this was a tactical position more than a sincere belief. And only the latest serious economic crises, international isolation, and the terminal decline of the Janus-faced empire (Tlostanova 2003),[2] which is now hastily swapping its masks, shifted the situation in a drastic way. As a result, the Central Asian and Caucasus states and regions, some of which are still formally part of the Russian Federation, started looking for other partners and coalitions, including those in the Middle and Far East—the partners, which before used to be kept in reserve as the association with the old Russian and Soviet metropolis was simpler and, possibly, safer.

In the non-European post-Soviet former colonies and in the Russian Federation itself, art seems to be among the very few remaining ways to reflect critically on the intersection of the decolonial and de-Sovietizing impulses. No postcolonial or much less decolonial revisionist models have been allowed to go into circulation, and in the context of the Russian Federation's annexation of Crimea in 2014, theorists, politicians, and activists have been cut off from the use of any such potentially dissident tools. In the latest Russian reactionary wave, the old familiar logic is reproduced: as in the time of Leo Tolstoy, art, once again, fulfills the function of the missing, strangled, or co-opted critical social theory, philosophy, and political activism. The list of artists performing the important tasks of critical reflection includes, among others, Evgeny Antufiev, Aslan Gaisumov, Vladimir Dubossarsky, Shifra Kazhdan, Sergey and Tatyana Kostrikov, Taus Makhacheva, Anton Nikolayev, Anatoly Osmolovsky, Pyotr Pavlensky, Timofey Radya, Egor Rogalev, Anna Titova, and Alexander Vinogradov.

The most doomed situation is in Russia itself, which has suffered under the imperial difference syndrome for several centuries (certainly long before it attempted to build state Socialism). Russia strove to fit into the logic of catching up and tried to build a separate Socialist modernity, with its own coloniality sharing the main premises of modernity at large, such as racism, Orientalism, progressivism, the rhetoric of salvation, a fixation on newness, asymmetrical divisions of labor—that is, generally the coloniality of being, gender, knowledge, and sensibility. The Russian empire was dominated culturally, technologically, intellectually, and in other ways by the core European countries, yet it subsumed other peripheral spaces, making it a clear case of semiperipherality.

The lighter side of Soviet modernity was grounded in ideological and social differences that were used to build human hierarchies. Its darker colonial side mostly reiterated the nineteenth-century racist clichés and human taxonomies mixed with hastily adapted historical materialist dogmas. Today's Russia is still nonhomogeneous, and the restarting of its "parade of sovereignties" is threatening to dismantle the country forever. Secessionism inside the Russian Federation is not only ethnic, cultural, and religious but also clearly economic, as it is linked with an uneven regional redistribution of resources, with the pillage of the provinces in favor of Moscow, with the articulation and development of often militant regional identities and ultimately, with their urge to become independent. The latter tendency can be witnessed in the cases of Altay, Tatarstan, the Volga region, and Yakutia, as well as parts of Siberia, and has already become the focus of attention of several contemporary art activists.

The concept of internal colonization, which has become popular thanks to Alexander Etkind's book *Internal Colonization: Russia's Imperial Experience* (2011), is now acquiring a different and less historically and contextually bound meaning, which Etkind himself may have not intended. He compared Russian serfs to African American slaves and Amerindians, pointing out the lack of racial difference between masters and serfs in the case of Russia and claiming that the category of "estate" acted as a substitute for race. Rather the whole Russian model can be viewed as a case of zoological coloniality, following the nineteenth-century Siberian dissident Afanasy Shchapov (1906), to whom Etkind devoted one of the best chapters of his book. Shchapov meant a parallel annihilation of fur-providing animals and the indigenous people who were forced to hunt those animals, under pain of death, during the early colonization of Siberia. Today this model of dehumanizing and equating human lives with mere instruments of thoughtless natural resource extraction covers the entire population of the Russian Federation, regardless of our ethnic/racial, class, and religious belonging.

Once again, the Janus-faced empire is trapped between its two masks: the servile visage that, following Frantz Fanon's logic (1967), could be identified as Russian faces and Western masks; and a patronizing mask meant for Russia's own, non-European eastern and southern colonies and former colonies. Today this configuration is complicated and changed in a new geopolitical situation in which the lives of ordinary citizens of all religions and ethnicities are seen as dispensable. At the present moment when a handful of Russian state oligarchs have already completely pillaged the remnants of the Soviet economy (which was not the most efficient but still was created by the collective efforts of the Soviet people, not by a handful of properly connected tycoons) and pumped the profit into their foreign bank accounts, and when oil and gas production stopped to be sufficiently gainful, they turned to looting the deprived population as the only remaining source of easy profit and to physical elimination of both the weak and the dissatisfied.

I Come from Nowhere, or Back to the Same Sensibility after Twenty-Five Years

Today, dwelling in a quiet Swedish town I am often reflecting on the fact that more than half of my life took place in the post-Soviet waiting and survival room from which there is obviously no way out and that has slowly turned into a place to wait for the other world beyond life and death. This is probably the main human existential result of twenty-five post-Soviet years. I indicate them with two very personal milestones which nevertheless are directly connected with the gist of the post-Soviet human condition.

In the year of the Soviet Union's quiet collapse I was an exchange student in the United States. After my study abroad program I was going back home and I realized that I had a passport from a nonexistent state: the USSR. Certainly I was allowed to leave the United States,—albeit with an ironic smile—and let into the newly established Russian Federation with a habitual gloomy suspicion. Moreover, Soviet foreign passports remained valid for almost ten years after the collapse because there were simply too many passport blanks previously produced with a typical Soviet imperial grandeur and planning economy zeal. They had to be used in spite of the fact that no such country existed any more. But while I was standing in the passport control line at the poorly lit and dirty Sheremetyevo International Airport—which was only starting to be filled with exiles and refugees, the bits and pieces of empire striving to break free from its still tenacious hands—I suddenly felt that for us, the holders of such passports, the very passage of time had changed. The sea of time almost palpably went around us and left us behind, discarded in some cases as if we were fish suffocating on a dry, sandy shore. Twenty-five years have passed, and today the same sense of disintegration is clearly in the air once again. And I have no idea what will await me if I decide to use my now Russian passport sometime in the near future to visit my place of birth. Could recent history repeat itself so soon, especially since we have never learned its lessons?

The past twenty-five post-Soviet years have been marked by a strange reverse logic for former inhabitants of the USSR, a logic that falls outside the usual modern progressivism, typical for the relations of the global North and South. We woke up one day to find ourselves in a new condition that was chosen for us by someone else. It was a condition of a dinosaur that somehow did not die in due time and had to languish in the back yards of history, which at that point indeed seemed to have reached its climax and come to a standstill in the eternal consumerist paradise. Yet even those Soviet people who honestly believed in their opportunity to change and join the world, and who hastily started working toward this condition, soon realized that the road from our own history into the real world was quite long and hard, and maybe it was even a dead-end.

We woke up to a new reality of multiple dependencies and increased unfreedoms in which the previous Soviet unfreedom was not at all lifted, but, on the contrary soon acquired new forms that combined economic exploitation with the lack of rights and renewed ideological control. That is, although the external forms changed, conditions remained the same in their repressive essence. In fact, it was a story of the suddenly cancelled Socialist modernity that left its voluntary and involuntary participants and agents in ruin and unable to rejoin history. According to one respondent in *Secondhand Time* (2013, 91), by the Nobel Prize–winning author Svetlana Alexievich, "Socialism has ended, but we are still here." The post-Soviet people became equivalents of a losing race and bound to disappear or merge with the global South.

The Soviet immigrant Boris Groys, now a social and art theorist in Germany, stresses the paradoxical direction of the path taken by most postsocialist countries: "The post-Communist subject travels the same route as described by the dominating discourse of cultural studies—but he or she travels this route in the opposite direction, not from the past to the future, but from the future to the past; from the end of history . . . back to historical time. Post-Communist life is life lived backward, a movement against the flow of time" (Groys 2008, 155). Groys thinks that the state Socialist modernity in a sense was a leap *against* the course of the world history, an attempt to transcend it. The more difficult and crashing it became for us to be later sent back to the usual course, speed and direction of history and to change the radical Socialist progressivist model to a milder version of the forever unattainable Western ideal; why we continue to plod slowly and endlessly along instead of leaving the drudgery behind and leaping into the new and wonderful future in one jump. This shift was interpreted by many people as a way backward, and used by the neo-imperial ideologues as a justification of their revanchist appetites. In purely religious or secular Soviet forms, the Russian empire had always aimed at taking a revenge for the losing battle with the West and ultimately erasing the imperial difference.

The state of being expelled from history reiterated the general logic of modernity, with its habitual operation of translating geography into chronology (Mignolo 2000) and assigning whole groups of people living in the non-Western spaces to other times or, rather, positioning them outside the only sanctioned course of time and the only appropriate way of life. Yet in the post-Soviet case, it was not the downtrodden premodern "savages" on whom the Western modernity could practice its civilizing discourses. Rather, it was an other state Socialist modernity which failed and was subsequently rendered nonviable, while its voluntary and involuntary practitioners had to be instructed on how to become fully modern (in the only remaining neoliberal way) and, ultimately, fully human. The progressivist paradigm has had an inbuilt feature of always keeping a sufficient lag between the modernizing catching-up ex-Socialists and the first rate Western/ Northern subjects.

Soon it became clear that post-Soviet people seemingly sent to the end of the queue, in fact, were simply squeezed out of history, because the catching-up would never end in overtaking. We found ourselves in the void, in a problematic locale inhabited by problem people. And it was this situation of having nothing to lose that shaped today's dangerous postimperial *ressentiment*. Yet in speaking about a generalized postsocialist person, Groys neglects the colonial difference inside the external imperial difference— the darker side of (post-)Soviet modernity marked by Orientalism, racism, othering, and forced assimilation—and indirectly denies the fact that Soviet progressivism meant one thing for Russians and something else for Uzbeks and Georgians. Thus, their present trajectories cannot be parallel or identical by definition.

As stated earlier, the hidden Russian inferiority complexes typical of external imperial difference have led from time to time to lapses into imperial jingoism and revanchism that have now reached an extreme manifestation in which a new political identity is being made out of stigmatization. In other words, Russia is effectively saying, "If the West calls me barbarous, I will behave so." In the past several years, this sentiment has been accentu-

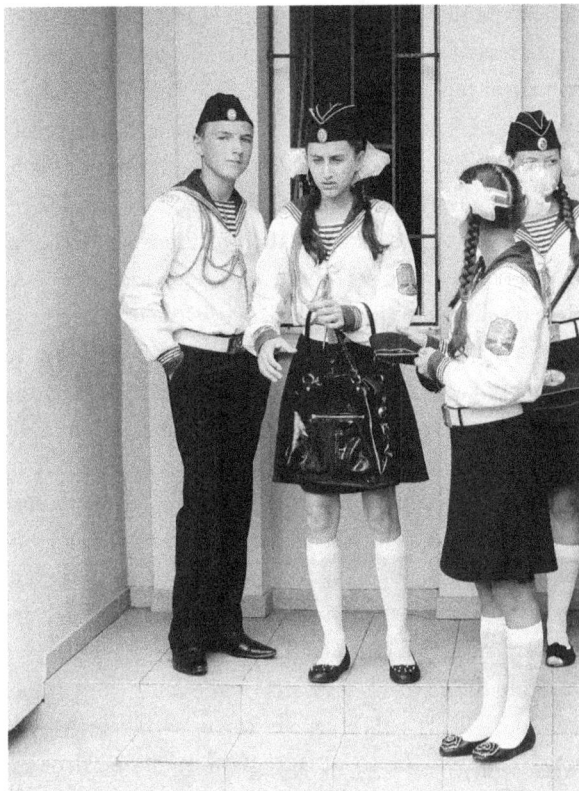

FIG. INTRO.1 Egor Rogalev, *Situation No. 2*. Odessa, 2011. Archival photographic print in various editions; dimensions variable. From the photo series Synchronicity. Courtesy of the artist.

ated and cultivated more and more frequently in the official Russian discourses, stressing that Russia is not Europe, and elevating the previously marginal neo-Eurasianism to an almost official state ideology.

The Russian Wolf in Postcolonial Sheep's Clothing

In its present hysterically aggressive stage, Russia is trying to jump out of the catching-up model, in which it has existed at least since the seventeenth-century reign of Peter the Great, and trying to make the world stop viewing the imperial difference as a colonial difference, thus turning itself once again into a respectable partner for the global North. This very impulse is quite deceiving as it does not try to question the logic of modernity/coloniality as such, but merely alters Russia's position in it. This humble goal is camouflaged as anticolonial pathos and a critique of the West, which is skillfully used by the Russian administration to brainwash a population that is already distracted by serious economic and social problems and marked by "defuturing" tendencies (Fry 2011, 21). This imperial appropriation of postcolonial rhetoric also targets the Western left, who reflect on the Russian situation from safe positions and often praise President Vladimir Putin's escapades for their anti-Americanism. However, that position remains blind to the fate of those at whose expense the dangerous neo-imperial attacks are made. It erases political and economic repression, increased poverty, completely destroyed social state, and the looming extinction of a huge country that has become a hostage to its insane and reckless regime.

It is not possible to separate the Russian face from its underside. And the same way as modernity is not possible without its darker colonial side, the second-rate imperial démarches and efforts to carve a safer space in the modern/colonial system are impossible without infringing on human rights and looting their own populations, the would-be citizens who are objectified, once again, as the instruments of the zoological economy. As a trade commodity, fur was simply replaced for a while by oil; now it is the turn of the population itself to be sacrificed and skinned by the state. After the last bits of property are taken away from the animalized subjects of the collapsing regime, the depopulated territory most likely will cease to be interesting to anybody—most of all, to its own power elites. Therefore, the ugly and scary mask of the imperial Janus, which once was turned in the direction of the non-European colonies, today is turned toward every citizen, whether they are applauding the neo-imperial rhetoric or prefer their refrigerators to television sets.

The Russian imperial difference, characterized by the empire's status on the second tier and the constant presence of stronger Western rivals, has generated multiple colonial differences among its colonized subjects, which might actually find colonization by a first-rate empire more attractive.[3] It is important to understand how this configuration is evolving in the world in relation to other, more global processes; how the post-Soviet people revolt against an obvious injustice of the modern power asymmetry but often do so in dangerous rightist, revanchist forms that are carefully planted by state ideologues to later make food for powder out of its own citizens in neoimperial military operations such as the infamous denied war with Ukraine.[4] Those who disagree also find themselves in a paradoxical situation both inside and outside the country: while abroad, we are often still held responsible for the sins of Putin's regime, while at home we are branded as a "fifth column" and persecuted as traitors and foreign agents.

Today the Russian Federation's state ideologues are desperately feeding the impoverished population with an unappetizing soup of discourses drawn from imperial narratives that are quite different both contextually and temporally. They range from almost theocratic statist models of sacred geography superseding geopolitics, grounded in the sanctification of the state and the ruler and aggressive territorial expansionism masked by various spiritual justifications, to revivalism of the Socialist and, particularly, Stalinist "grandeur," which attempts to glue disjointed and emaciated people spread over a gigantic and unmanageable territory together via memories of military valor and sports and space-exploration accomplishments of the Soviet époque. But efforts to reanimate national and imperial mythological consciousness have not been particularly successful. Their main axis—the invented interconnection between Russia's territorial vastness and its grandeur—is increasingly shattered by growing secessionist sensibilities and the development of regional identities and imaginaries in various parts of the country. They feel themselves as the new old colonies of Moscow, and more and more actively discuss different possibilities of separation and survival on their own or with the help of different partners—from Western Europe to China and Iran. One more imperial card that is now being played is the Russian language as a unifying force. Appeals to a linguistic unity of the "Russian world" are present in various neo-imperial agendas—right, left and centrist—from Alexander Dugin to present day National Bolsheviks.

Another recurrent element of Russian imperial mythology is the false narrative of Russia as a savior of suffering nations. This myth is still successfully employed in imperial propaganda for both Russians and a number of presumably liberated people, such as those in several countries of the former Yugoslavia and in Bulgaria, who juxtapose the imagined Orthodox Slavic community with a demonized Ottoman yoke. Russia's annexation of Crimea in 2014 and the tragic and shameful events that followed in Ukraine and Syria (and the preceding neoimperial war in Georgia) were grounded in similar false arguments of defending the Russians or their brother nations living in someone else's territory or destroying civilians under the pretext of fighting terrorism. At first, many post-Soviet people took this rationale at face value, having fished out of their unconscious the all too familiar conservative and revanchist servility and a sickening allegiance to those in power, which still lie very close to the surface. Yet today's Soviet renaissance is another simulacrum, an empty shell with no meaning, a playful revival of Stalinist Russia, where mortal fear and deadly conviction are normalized once again, but go hand in hand with cynical corruption, demagogic invectives, and typical arguments of timeservers living out of their suitcases. Artists were the first to detect and critically address this falseness, such as the Ukrainian poet Serhiy Zhadan, the Russian writer Vladimir Sorokin, the directors Kirill Serebrennikov and Andrey Zvyagintsev, the Georgian novelist Zaza Burchuladze, and the Crimean film director and activist Oleg Sentsov, and others.

The Black Legend, Russian/Soviet-Style

In our effort to understand the evolution of the external imperial difference today, we should take into account that at every stage of its evolution it has been marked by the logic of the Leyenda Negra (black legend),[5] which was well tested in the rivalry between the British and Spanish empires. "Black legendism" also flourishes in Russia today, and no one has yet attempted to problematize it. The Janus-faced empire represents itself as good, spiritual, kind, and fair, in opposition to its Western and non-Western rivals. This is expressed in Russia's habitual stigmatization of the double standards of the West. Yet these accusations themselves are grounded in morally dubious and logically flawed assumptions that exempt Russia from the zone of responsibility for its own actions—that is, if the West does not comply with its own laws and rules and if it violates human rights, why should Russia bother to comply with international law? However, on the global scale, it does not matter who violates human rights—European countries, the United States, or Russia, who could trigger a global disaster. What does matter is how we can learn to live together in this world without infringing on other people's rights and then justifying it by pointing our accusing fingers at others.

Strangely enough, the logic of self-justification by accusing others is supported by many leftist intellectuals who do not seem to be aware of the fact that discarding the legitimacy of international law—however imperfect it is as such or how irregularly it is implemented—could easily lead us to destruction and violence for their own sake or as an intimidation tool. But does it really make sense to blackmail the international community with constant military threats? If so, we will soon have a Hobbesian society of war of all against all. Or maybe we already live in that society. Would it not be better to abstain from claiming that everyone is equal in violating the laws and instead act maturely by trying to formulate laws, and global mechanisms for their implementation, that would not infringe on anyone's rights? We have to find a global way of negotiating our common future on this planet in order to have any future at all. And the global coloniality needs to be globally dismantled instead of trying to carve a better space in its perverse hierarchy or paying it back with equal violence and lawlessness.

Alas, the external imperial difference continues to reproduce the black legend logic at all stages of its evolution. Thus, Russia applies a technique of looking for Western faults while ignoring or shadowing its own deficiencies. This has occurred throughout history and could take constructive forms of borrowing and improving the Western accomplishments. As the semiotician Yuri Lotman has demonstrated, with the Byzantine Empire acting as an equivalent of the West, Russian thinkers claimed a better understanding and implementation of Greek doctrine than the original Orthodox Christian Church. Later, Russian interpreters of the French enlightenment once again claimed they better understood the main principles than the French. The Bolsheviks also borrowed their main tenets from Western socialist and communist doctrines and then altered them to suit their purposes and presented this alteration as an improvement (Lotman 2002, 273).

The false mythology of the Russian/Soviet imperial liberating mission has also acquired the form of a "black legend" and was grounded in the opposition of Russia, presumably helping other nations break free of evil and mercenary Western empires, which were oppressing poor people in India, Africa, and the Americas. The Russian religious philosopher Vladimir Solovyev pointed this out in 1888 by drawing attention to the double standards of the Janus-faced empire:

> We wanted to liberate Serbia and Bulgaria, but at the same time we continued to oppress Poland. This system of oppression is bad in itself, but it becomes much worse due to the crying discrepancy with liberating ideals and disinterested help that Russian politics has always claimed to be its style and its exclusive right. These politics are necessarily drenched in lying and hypocrisy that take away any prestige. . . . One cannot—with perfect impunity—write on his banner the freedom of all Slavs and other people while simultaneously taking national freedom away from the Poles; religious freedom away from the Uniats and Russian religious dissenters; [and] civil rights away from the Jews. (Solovyev 2002, 247–48)

These words are still true today. In accordance with this double standard, Russia continues to "liberate" nations in order to colonize them or make them useful in establishing or reconfirming its geopolitical dominance. The lack of any collective repentance or massive intellectual de-imperialization are contributing to Russia's defeat today.

The Perishable Soviet Renaissance Minus the Future

The fact that we cannot bury the past and start living in the present is linked not only to our acquiescence to being made into victims once again but also to our inability and unwillingness to think critically and finally shelve Soviet modernity/coloniality in an archive or museum. Easily revived inferiority complexes, together with memories of imperial grandeur and the deification of power in its personalized forms that equate the ruler, the state, and the country, are immediately channeled by imperial ideologues and their mass-media henchmen to prolong the agony of the regime and prevent the collapse of the falling empire for a little longer.

The reanimation of the Soviet modernity project—which in essence, if not in its form continued the aggressive messianism of Russian Orthodoxy—is being used to extend the fragile status quo. And the belt-tightening rhetoric with universal justice as its fake goal seems to switch on in the collective unconscious memories of earlier liberating discourses: from the biblical "the last shall be first" to *L'Internationale*'s "We are nothing; let us be all." But an important difference, or even a deliberate deception, is at work here: no one today is promising happiness even in the distant future, to say nothing of the possibility of any future per se. The Soviet discourse used to present the ideal future as an open and unrestrained utopia, at least until the mid-1960s when it became obvious that communism would not come any time soon and the Soviet ideology shifted toward the past.

Yet at the core of state Socialist utopianism for a long time stood the idea of universal happiness and consequently the happy future. It is true that way too soon utopia became sealed and exclusionary. But the social contract of the Soviet people was in many ways linked to this imagined future happiness that they were offered to exchange for the hardships and difficulties of their present. Today the belt-tightening rhetoric is not compensated any more by any promise of the universal happiness in near or distant future. What we are offered instead is merely a symbolic compensation in the form of phantasmal superiority. The worn out victory-in-defeat discourse and the inevitable post-apocalyptic triumph, in the Russian case are transferred entirely to the spiritual realm or even to hereafter. Those who do not believe in the other world ruin themselves by drink or leave this forcefully galvanized dead world for good.[6] It is not surprising therefore that the lion's share of artists, writers and film directors in contemporary Russia work with dystopian genres.

The favorite cliché of Russian media borrowed from one of President Putin's speeches, likens the country to a slave who after twenty-five years is finally getting up from his knees. Yet few options are being left open for the slave who has been deceived into believing that economic stagnation and lack of prospects for the future mean liberation from the West. It is really a choice between the slow and miserable vegetation and survival in the shrinking and stagnant economy, and the all-too-familiar Russian "meaningless and merciless revolt" (Pushkin 1960, 387), which would be immediately suppressed by the masters. Therefore, the shelf life of false liberation discourses such as the Kremlin's current imitation of ideology is quite short.

Those who used to be nothing at all times—before the 1917 Revolution, in the USSR, under Yeltsin and Putin—are more and more aware of the deception of the false exchange imposed on them by those in power. But what can they really do, and how can they really influence the political, social, or any other sphere of life in Russia today? This bitter awareness of the impossibility to change anything is perhaps the most hopeless feature of contemporary Russian social and political reality. However, even the simplest consumerist and previously pro-status quo minds have started to demonstrate signs of doubt. Those who were ready to exchange their rights and freedoms for a relative economic well-being and the infamous deadening stability, which was replaced far too quickly with state-of-emergency rhetoric, are not happy anymore, and this emerging new reality cannot be ignored.

When I was writing the first draft of this introduction, one of the central Moscow streets—Tverskaya—was blocked by protesters. They were not hungry medical doctors or teachers, starving retirees or miners as it happened in the 1990s. They were relatively well-off middle-class people who took bank loans in hard currency because the interest rate was lower than the ruble mortgage. With the rapid devaluation of the ruble, in which their salaries are paid, they have lost everything. One can accuse them of greed and say that this is their own problem. However, it is revealing that these middle-class victims of devaluation understand the direct relationship between the state's predatory politics and their own personal problem with the banks. A video shown often on social media networks features a desperate woman wearing a mink coat yelling from a picket line across Tverskaya, which leads to the Kremlin, "Maybe we should give Crimea back—do we really need it?" Crimea is indeed needed only symbolically, and the destiny of the Crimean people once again demonstrates Russia's typical treatment of human beings as expendable material.[7] It is more important to destroy the enemy than to save the hostages, civilians or soldiers. The lacking rights paradigm and dispensability of human lives have remained the main features of the Russian imperial difference.

To describe the nature of nationalism, Benedict Anderson (1983, 86) applied the metaphor of the narrow skin of the nation-state that is too small to cover the body of the old empire. In the case of the Russian/Soviet empire, this metaphor was further twisted as in the end the old skin was removed and the new one never appeared. Or rather, a number of the pieces of the old empire attempted to reuse fragments of the old (Soviet) skin by renovating it with ersatz ethnic-national ornaments but, in fact, keeping the old Marxist stagist paradigm intact. (A good example is Uzbekistan, whose recently deceased President Islam Karimov managed to preserve a hybrid Soviet-feudal regime for almost three decades.) Russia itself has long been in a vulnerable and unstable position, unable to weave itself new clothes or recycle its old ones. Soon it became clear that the bombastic innovation initiatives always clash against the persistent Soviet-Russian rigid structures and post-Soviet cynical corruption, leading to nothing. Today the half-collapsed empire is being hastily covered with this worn out cloth marked by a serious cognitive dissonance of harsh neoliberal logic, dusted with fundamentalist nationalist and imperial rhetoric which is worded in a distinctly populist way (Matveyev 2016).

There is no teleology and no point of arrival anymore. And no one is ready to suffer in this world or in their lifetime for the sake of some abstract utopian happiness of the future generations or even of some otherworldly bliss. The resource of waiting for the wonderful future in the conditions of present deprivation and humiliation is completely exhausted. History did not end after all; it bypassed us. The vastness of space almost always prevailed over time in Russian history (except during a few swooping and mobilizing efforts to force history to jump); today, the preeminence of wilderness that was never properly cultivated or tamed is coming forward once again. As post-Soviet Russia falls out of modernity, in its Western and Soviet versions, it is coming to a standstill.

Although the post-Soviet societies have lived in a state of crisis for the past twenty-five years, the present crisis is rapidly turning into a crisis of legitimacy in which epistemic, existential, and cultural—not just social, economic, and political—elements come forward, reinforcing anomie, dissociation, and extreme willy-nilly individualism among the inhabitants of the collapsing empire. This is a peculiar form of individualism that is grounded not in human or civic dignity or responsibility but in sheer physical survival of the poor and deprived as they come face to face with the hostile world and repressive state-oligarchic capitalism. In spite of all propagandistic clichés and false myths imposed from the inside and outside, today's post-Soviet everyman is not the proverbial Socialist collectivist or a proponent of the Russian *sobornost* as a utopian "communal" ideal, opposed to liberal "commonwealth" and Marxist "commons." These confused people, who just a few months ago proudly wore their patriotic Saint George's ribbons and were capable of uniting only against someone but not for anything, suddenly are ready to fight collectively for economic and social well-being and demand that the power they have always supported finally fulfill its part of the social contract.

The inflated paroxysms of patriotism by the dying Russian state are in fact efforts to fill a vacuum of beliefs with empty semantics and artificially unite the dissociated masses under the banner of some fragile collective identity, even though they share little more than growing repression, common territory, and language. Such enforced reunifications are tactical and essentially short term, which the imperial ideologues realize better than anyone else. The infusion of neoimperial ideology and policies are needed only until those in power can finish their marauding projects and escape, leaving the nonviable *homo post-soveticus* to perish and make room for other communities.

In *Secondhand Time*, Alexievich attempts to understand what constitutes our post-Soviet existential condition. In interview after interview, she reveals recycled, secondhand beliefs and experiences that do not help to build anything new in the ruins. Today Alexievich's metaphor will acquire even more sinister overtones because the secondhand time of the Socialist modernity is being miraculously resurrected in the most sickening elements of the authentic Soviet reality. Yet it is a repetition with a difference: in the original Soviet world, everything was deadly serious, including the peoples' genuine, and hence more powerful and terrifying, feelings and beliefs. Soviet people went easily to their doom for the grand ideals, however false. Today's Russian citizens, by contrast, are offered only a bad theatrical

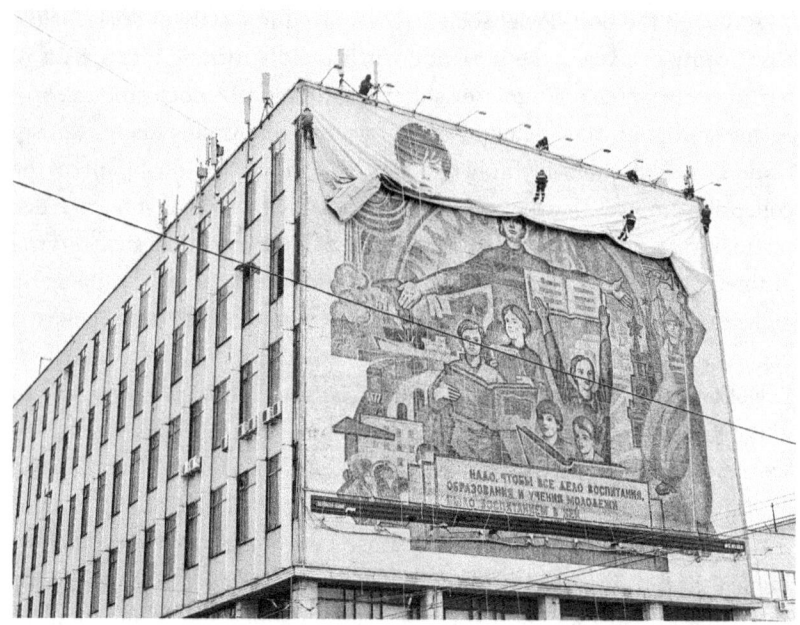

FIG. INTRO.2 Egor Rogalev, *Situation No. 29*. Moscow, 2011. Archival photographic print in various editions; dimensions variable. From the photo series Synchronicity. Courtesy of the artist.

performance—a cocktail of Stalinism and fascism with strong Orthodox Christian and fundamentalist nationalist ferment.

The Soviet utopia always retained a powerful element of messianism and the utopian teleology of building a new and wonderful world. Consequently, future stood in the center of its grand narrative. It was a special future equally happy for everyone and built to last forever, even if the Soviet state wanted to make everyone happy by force without asking their opinion. This hope supported the exhausted people for a while in the 1990s, allowing to believe in the possibility of future changes and the necessity of enduring hardship for the sake of the wonderful tomorrow. The revival of imperial rhetoric today cannot persuade anyone because it lacks an essential feeling of stability, the confidence of coming and staying forever in which the Soviet époque was grounded before. Today's return of the Soviet rhetoric is a case of a "bad faith" from the start. It is a conscious self-deceptive technique or, in Lewis Gordon's understanding, a rethinking of the Sartrean *mauvaise-foi*: "bad faith which is such because it in effect is an effort to perform a variety of contradictions the consequence of which requires lying to ourselves, making ourselves believe what we don't believe, using our freedom to deny it, asserting the very human effort at human evasion" (Gordon 2000, 157).

The present appeals to tighten belts or die in the service of someone else's interests in the multiple wars in which Russia is engaging as it follows its petty imperialist and short-term tactical agendas and bullies the West with fake criminal style hysteria are needed only to distract attention from one more episode of money laundering or economic failure. These appeals, however, almost never call for a wonderful future in any foreseeable time or in this material world, much less for any egalitarian future as it was the case in the USSR—at least on paper. The present administration realizes that no one would believe in such promises any more. The wonderful future is cancelled, and by way of compensation we are offered to be happy with the symbolic victory over the imagined enemies, and practice spiritual and religious superiority and aggressive Messianic zeal, uncompensated with anything in this material world. People deprived of any future, do not cherish their lives and therefore are easily manipulated and become potentially dangerous. Not surprisingly, many discourses popular in contemporary Russia revolve around eschatological premonitions with an accent on the dream of a new paradise with its center in Russia. In fact, this is the logic of a fanatical sect whose victims and hostages in this case are the whole population of a still large postimperial country which is sick with a syndrome of the lacking future and missing hope.

We are not even sure if this future would ever come. But what is to be done in such a situation, is something everyone decides for themselves. Knowing that victory is impossible and our efforts to fight are doomed, at least in the near future, makes some of us leave the country and others reconcile and busy themselves with mere survival. But there are also those who continue to speak up and act against, knowing that they will never win yet also rejecting the continuation of the slavish existence. Even today there are spheres in which decolonial thinkers are able to continue their internal activism, which is destructive to the existing deadening system and aimed at future existential resurgence—and, eventually, the emergence of a freer individual who can enter a dynamic correlational network with other people and the nonhuman world. This is a meticulous and step-by-step work on decolonizing people's minds and bodies and offering them different options and various optics of looking at the world and at themselves from the critical edge of modernity and coloniality. This could potentially lead to independent thinking, and to new coalitions grounded not in ideology or stale geopolitics, but in other alter-global modes of thinking and being marked by a realization of our common destiny as humans and striving to build a world in which no one would be an "other" anymore.

Art as an Effective Decolonial Force

This book focuses on a specific kind of decoloniality linked with perceptive mechanisms of aesthesis and further shaping not only of aesthetic and ethical but also, inevitably, of political stances and agency that may become powerful mechanisms in decolonizing thinking, being, sensing, and corporality. After analyzing various spheres of decoloniality in the past decade, I have come to the conclusion that contemporary activist art that is closely connected with corporality and affectivity—and, consequently, with the intersection and problematizing of epistemic and ontological links—is the area in which the most effective decolonial models emerge. It is this sphere that gives some hope for the post-Soviet future.

Unfortunately, the nature of the post-Soviet regimes—and particularly of Russia—is for the state either to crush or to co-opt any direct forms of social and political protest. Activists who do make it into public space are generally unable to offer radically decolonizing agendas. Instead, they continue to exist within the old logic of political parties and movements, which tend to be highly ineffective in the struggle against global and local forms of coloniality. Moreover, openly political movements are immediately persecuted, and critical social and political thought—even that which is purely theoretical—is banned, marginalized, or forced into exile.

Activism-cum-art—or "artivism" (Nikolayev 2011)—practices are becoming more effective in the conditions of the impasse and stagnation of most social protest movements unable to influence the economic or political decisions. The artistic influence seems less immediate than any open social or political dissent, yet it slowly works for the implementation of the future radical changes through altering our thinking, and setting our consciousness free from the global neoliberal or local jingoistic brainwashing. Art in its visual, verbal and synthetic forms remains a crucial intersection of being and knowledge and it is in the sphere of aesthesis untouched by any normative aesthetic distortions that the most promising decolonizing models start to emerge.

Activist art does not, however, exist in inherently safe space. It is also subject to repression. But it has at least two advantages: art is metaphorical by definition and therefore slips more easily out of power's grip; and the vagueness of metaphors, along with their ability to multiply often contradictory meanings allows artists adjusting to new censorship and double-think situations.

According to Judith Butler (1997, 15), censorship is always ineffective and unsuccessful from the start because any utterance is always multi-semantic, particularly in the realms of art, fiction, film, and the humanities, where the multiplicity of interpretations is axiomatic. At the same time, open protests against censorship do not always solve the problem as they cannot shatter the system as such. On the contrary, we then build ourselves into the system and play according to its rules, instead of overcoming the system through its subversion from the inside or delinking from the system and creating something independent. The advantage of art is that it is able to discuss the utmost questions without sliding into obvious propaganda and open and univocal political engagement.

Indirect protest tactics and strategies of undermining power structures from within have become well developed in postcolonial, posttotalitarian, and postdictatorship art. Even Soviet censorship was an interactive process, grounded in a peculiar and complex complicity of the censor and the censored. Censorship obviously "inhibited and provoked . . . authors" (Levine 1995, 2). It also acted as an impetus for stylistic innovation among artists and helped develop in audiences a heightened sensitivity to the hidden and the implied. The censor is always tormented by the "monologic terror of indeterminacy" (Holquist 1994, 22) because it is not possible to fix meanings once and for all, to cement interpretation in unequivocal aesthetic, political, or ethical ways. Multiplicity of interpretations, complex interconnection of negation and assertion in any censorship, and reiteration as its main principle, lead to restating of the very utterances censorship seeks to banish.

There are certainly many opposite examples of the obvious repressions against the activist artists such as Pyotr Pavlensky, Pussy Riot, activist art festival Media Impact, or Vyacheslav Akhunov. But art still has more chances to avoid the punishment of repressive systems and offer a wider specter of interpretations and opinions than any purely political and rationalized forms of protest. In contrast with social theory, the immediate and often nonrational affective form of art, is able to better and faster convey the vague and undefined sensibilities of protest and affirmation of another way of being that social theorists cannot formulate using their bulky and slowly changing methodological apparatus—or that they are afraid to formulate as they remain loyal to their rigid disciplinary frames.

Obviously, contemporary art seldom appeals to mass audiences even if the majority of artists I will refer to in the book are far from being elitist or living in any ivory tower. They are able to actively engage with the critically thinking part of the educated and responsible people, who still reside in the postsocialist countries. These are the people who attend exhibitions of contemporary art and are ready to discover something new and relate it to their own experience. Such art initiatives are often closely linked with social and political movements and protests never completely merging with them.

This book offers one possible view of decolonization in post-Soviet aesthesis. I hope that, in the future, more decolonial reflections on the post-Soviet imaginary will be done via other spheres that are not necessarily connected with art. However, art is the most promising sphere in the realization of decoloniality in the present post-Soviet space.

Beyond the TV-Fridge Dichotomy

The art and artists discussed in this volume offer the exhausted post-Soviet person a way beyond the dichotomy of the TV set and the refrigerator, a way into a different dimension in which there are other notions and beliefs besides bread and game. They are not proposing to place the TV set inside the empty refrigerator, but rather to delink from this false, imposed logic and see that there are many other options in the world and some of them we can even initiate ourselves and start doing it already now. In this regard, the post-Soviet condition must not be seen as a lamentation of the lost paradise, but rather as a way to re-existence in a changing world in which many worlds would correlate and where the experience of Socialist modernity and its specific trajectory would shape one of the possible open models, intersecting but never entirely merging with others, and where the previous hierarchical relations of the state, the market and the artists would finally give place to other forms of communication, praxis and production of meanings. The art of the postsocialist world remains an effective means of such a collective cathartic therapy, which is likely to help post-Soviet citizens better understand ourselves and our place in the multiple and complex world in the making and never again slide into the vicious circle of forever dependent existence.

CHAPTER ONE

The Decolonial Sublime

For the post-Soviet human condition that I attempted to sketch briefly in the introduction, contemporary artivism grounded in decolonization of the affective sphere and in liberating aesthesis from the limitations of aesthetics, is particularly important and promising for the future. But first, what is meant by "aesthesis," and what is the difference between aesthetics and aesthesis? The term "aesthetics" was coined by Alexander Baumgarten (1750) to indicate a shift from sensibility to a taste in good art with a specific material and market value, and to a mode of articulation among various forms of agency, production, perception, and thinking. Aesthetics was a new institutionalized philosophical, moral, cultural, and social sphere, which around the early nineteenth century, according to Jacques Rancière (2009), shifted the previous representative regime of art to a contradictory aesthetic one, gradually leading to the demise of art as such, to its dissolving and merging with other activities. Rancière stresses that aesthetics was born during the French Revolution and therefore was bound up with equality, a democratic and liberating spirit that also signaled the future deterioration of art that was grounded in a destruction of previous artistic hierarchies, a dissolving of boundaries between art and life, and also a shift in relations between the passive sensibility and an active understanding of art (Rancière 2009, 37).

Rancière (2009, 49) addresses the present reconfiguration of the political in aesthetic forms and conferring on art the capacity to become an instrument of "reframing a sense of community and mending the social bond and time that binds together practices, forms of visibility, and patterns of intelligibility." Conceptualizing his idea of the community of sense as "a certain cutting out of space," Rancière (2009, 31, 49) claims that "art does not do politics by reaching the real. It does it by inventing fictions that challenge the existing distribution of the real and the fictional. . . . Fiction invents new communities of sense: that is to say, new trajectories between what can be seen, what can be said, and what can be done." It is hard to reanimate the concept of community in such conditions without equating it to the liberal understanding of the commonwealth or the Marxist idea of the commons. What often remains unaddressed are the models accentuating the aesthetic, sensual aspect of the political and social spheres that go beyond ideology as such. Rancière's take on aesthetics and politics remains within the universalized Western social and economic realm, but his ideas on contradictory political-aesthetic relations find parallels in a number of communal models of indigenous people and decolonial social movements grounded in intersectionality, which surpasses the simplified post-Marxist approach.

The term "aesthesis" has a longer implicit genealogy since it refers to an intrinsic human ability. "Aesthesis" literally means an ability to perceive through the senses and the process of sensual perception itself—visual, tactile, olfactory, gustatory, and so on. "Aesthesis" is more familiar to the general public as a Western postmodernist sociological term discussed by, among others, Michel Maffesoli in *The Time of the Tribes* (1988).[1] In this well-known book, Maffesoli starts and departs from an earlier phenomenological interpretation of aesthesis, as well as a number of nonorthodox sociological theories such as Vilfredo Pareto's model, to offer an aesthetic ground for his famous idea of the re-enchantment of the world.

However, Maffesoli's understanding—even if liberating and revolutionary for his time and context—is still limited as it is a critique of modernity from within, from a postmodernist position that is selectively correcting some of modernity's features but leaving the core and, particularly, its darker colonial side intact. Maffesoli understands aesthesis as a process of total aestheticization of the lifeworld in the collective consciousness of a tribe (a reunification of ethics and aesthetics). He means a critique of rationality and its replacement with intuitivism, sensuality, and emotional responses and also a critique of individualism and its replacement with new tribalism and group consciousness. Yet Maffesoli's tribes, as well as Deleuze and Guattari's (1993) war machine, are utopian constructions rather than real social groups. Although Maffesoli assumed that the total aestheticization of the lifeworld leads to the emergence of group ethics, empathy, and proxeny, and hence provides the possibility for an organic compromise between people, this assumption remains hypothetical. Moreover, the multitude of marginal communities with their presumable spirit of emotional complicity to which Maffesoli appeals, are still Western communities (such as hippies, anarchists, various contemporary experimental artists). They are unhappy with the system and capable of creating a rallying aesthesis as an immanent transcendence.

But in Maffesoli's interpretation, these new tribes are largely confined by contesting Western social movements and neo-avant-garde art. As is known, many such groups were dissatisfied with European philosophical traditions that did not allow one to move away from logocentrism. Therefore, the new tribalists started looking in the direction of Eastern and Amerindian cosmologies and various marginalized occult practices, which in itself was a form of colonization and appropriation of someone else's axiological legacy—a typical and well-rehearsed scenario of modernity. Moreover, this initially sincere revolutionary protest was soon tamed by the system. In fact, it was a doomed attempt to reform the system from within. The new tribalists' interest in the other remained largely an exotic desire to possess the other, not a genuine wish to learn more about this other. Such artificial affective excitement by means of alien cosmological instruments was predictably short-lived. And today, Maffesoli's old new tribes have given way to David Brooks's "Bobos" (2000)—a hybrid of the bohème and the bourgeoisie, in which aestheticization of protest has acquired safe and decorative forms. The neoliberal market and commodification mechanisms have easily infected the presumably autonomous artistic sphere and discredited and trivialized any naïve and honest ideals such as community and participation.

The present repoliticization of aesthetics takes place in rather bland and anonymous everyday forms of essentially apolitical practices pretending to be political, often with a focus on communicative and participatory practices and drives. A typical example is Nicolas Bourriaud's problematic relational aesthetics and his altermodern project (Bourriaud 2002b, 2009). Similarly to Maffesoli three decades ago, Bourriaud attempts to catch and reproduce the new sensibility assuming that globalization has successfully made this world homogenous and unified and its subjects have become identical and equal. Bourriaud sees the darker side of this homogeneity in the image of the globally standardizing capitalist system yet refuses to notice any power differences within it, condescendingly dismissing both postmodernism (as an outdated ideology and historical narrative) and postcolonialism and identity politics, which in his view have already fulfilled their obligations (Bourriaud 2009). In this respect he echoes the idea of post-Fordist dissolving of the previous power hierarchies through an emergence of radical democracy for the multiplicity of multitudes (Hardt and Negri 2005).

Obviously, this claim is being formulated once again from a familiar, disembodied Western vantage point, neglecting the growing asymmetries and hiding appropriation behind the concept of the Marxist commons. Accentuating creolization,[2] simplified and intensified contacts, migrations and journeys, and subtitles and translations as the landmarks of the new universal altermodern culture from which all artists, as Bourriaud claims, draw their techniques and devices, he once again appropriates concepts coming from non-Western theoretical paradigms, ignoring specific local contexts and histories of their emergence. Instead of Maffesoli's neo-tribalism and re-enchantment with the magic and irrational, Bourriaud offers a too banal fascination with Internet and computer technologies and computer metaphors such as "user-friendliness"; "do-it-yourself interactivity"; and the artist as engineer, programmer, or DJ, oversimplifying both contemporary reality and art (Bourriaud 2002a, 2009).

But let us delink from Maffesoli's understanding of aesthesis and rely on the decolonial interpretation of this category. With the emergence of explicit aesthetics in secular modernity, aesthesis was globally subsumed. It was a part of the wider process of colonization of being, knowledge, and perception that tagged the European past as premodern (traditional) and the non-European past and present as nonmodern and therefore nonhuman. This has led to strict formulations of what is beautiful and sublime, good and evil, and to the emergence of particular canonical structures and artistic genealogies.

Certainly the Western genealogy of thought revolted against such normative aesthetics long before Maffesoli. As a matter of fact, the philosophical revolt against ratio-centrism initiated by the end of the nineteenth century questioned the notorious "knowing subject," in Wilhelm Dilthey's formulation, and envisioned a being that not only thinks but also wills and feels (Dilthey 1991, 50). In many ways, Maffesoli follows in this path. Maffesoli's and decolonial interpretations of aesthesis share a problematizing of rationality and prescriptive aesthetic normativity, along with a focus on the collective experience as opposed to individual experience. Yet they do this from different geopolitical and corpo-political positions and trajectories of knowledge, perception, and being.

Decolonial aesthesis originates in the affective experience of those who have never been given a voice before and who also often have been (mis)-represented and appropriated by Maffesoli's new tribalists in the purely decorative form of noble savages and native informants, Calibans and Ariels. Such non-Western subjects are more sensitive to the corporeal dimensions of knowledge, perception, creativity, sexuality, and gender. In their experience, constructed bodily difference is constantly put forward, essentialized, and problematized, whereas they are seen or made invisible exclusively through their bodily difference.

Positioned at the intersection of ontology and epistemology, aesthesis acts as a mechanism to produce and regulate sensations; hence, it is inevitably linked with the body as an instrument of perception that mediates our cognition. Our bodies adapt to spaces through local histories—collective and personal. Cherríe Moraga and Gloria Anzaldúa (1981, 23) famously called this a "theory in the flesh," stressing the importance of the "physical realities of our lives," which "fuse to create a politics born out of necessity." Setting aesthesis free lets us delink from the dominant politics of knowledge, being, and perception, which is grounded in suppression of the geo-historical dimensions of affects and corporalities. Decolonial aesthesis grows out of the geopolitical and corpo-political position of the "outside created from the inside" (Dussel 1985), liberating us from often unconscious but persistent total control over sensations to which our bodies react, in Walter Mignolo's (2011) formulation. To do this, it is necessary to decolonize the knowledge that regulates aesthesis and the subjectivities that are controlled by Western modern/postmodern/altermodern aesthetics. Only then will it become possible to make a paradigmatic shift from often negative and destructive resistance to creative and life-asserting "re-existence," in Adolfo Albán Achinte's words (2006).

Albán Achinte explains that when a human being exists in the core of the colonial matrix as an other with no rights, for such a person an inclusion and an active reworking of odors, tastes, colors, and sounds of his or her ancestors and the remaking of systematically negated forms of interactions with the world—of being and perception—become a necessity, a sensual response of resistance and of building of one's own existence anew in defiance of coloniality (Albán Achinte 2009). Re-existence then becomes an effective decolonial strategy, (re-)creating the positive life models, sensations, and worlds that help to overcome the injustice and imperfection of the present world. Re-existence is far from a primordialist call to return to some essentialized and constructed authenticity. On the contrary, it is a way to relive the main elements of erased and distorted indigenous (or any other discarded) value systems while necessarily taking into account the temporal lag and experiences of struggle and opposition, compromises and losses, that have taken place. In other words, re-existence is not mere repetition; it is variation in which there is not only always a stable core but also a necessary creative element of difference, and hence of dynamics and change. What is at work here is a development of the native tradition in dialogue and in a constant argument with modernity. It is a complication and an enrichment of our perspective, a constant balancing on the verge— neither here nor there or simultaneously here, there, and elsewhere. Decolonial aesthesis lets our sensations, and consequently the assumptions we form on their basis, move forward and beyond the normative models of truth, beauty, and goodness, whether they are Western or native.

As a species, we share the ability to use simultaneously two different mechanisms of orientation and regulation of our behavior—the intellectual and the affective—intersecting them in the aesthetic sphere. Human mechanisms of perception may be universal, yet the manifestations of the affects and modes of our perception are always locally, historically, and culturally specific. Looking at the world from the "underside of modernity" (Dussel 1996, 21), decolonial artists and thinkers reflect on how they inhabit the colonial matrix of power, geographically and corpographically; how they respond to it aesthetically; and how they can overcome the persistent exoticization, appropriation, and condescending labeling (as "naive," "ethnic," "primitivist," "ornamentalist," "stylized," and so on) of their works within the predictable Western frames. By doing this they enact a process that is opposed to the naturalized (in Western modernity) delocalization and disembodiment of thinking and feeling, which in fact has hidden the provincialism of Western European aesthetic principles subsequently rendered universal.

Decolonial aesthesis, on the contrary, draws attention to the geopolitical location of aesthetic colonization and evolves, through practices of emancipation of experience, corporality, and affectivity, from the creative mechanisms, norms, and limitations of artificially delocalized and disembodied (post-)(alter)modern aesthetics. The decolonial emancipation of aesthesis leads to a reinvention of the concept of art itself, reuniting its ontological, ethical, political, and epistemic potential through subversion, disidentification, tricksterism, resistance, and re-existence. This makes intricate forms of contemporary aesthetic colonization, such as boutique multiculturalism and commodified exoticism, visible as ways to appropriate and tame the other and to exclude those who refuse to comply.

Contemporary aesthetic theory is predominantly post-Marxist and largely universalist. It tends to erase geopolitical and corpo-political affective differences. Hence, it stumbles against the same age-old problem of either taking the non-Western other to sameness or fetishizing its difference. When the same logic is applied to art, this dilemma once again takes the form of assimilating to the mainstream norm or being relegated to the non-Western ghetto of ethnic arts and crafts. W. E. B. Du Bois and his followers struggled with the ontological question of what it means to be a (human) problem (Gordon 2007). In the aesthetic sphere, this question changes into, "What does it mean to be an artist if you are seen as a problem? What kind of art you are expected to produce, and what can you do to escape the Procrustean bed of such prescribed definitions that want you to be either a mere craftsman or an object of someone else's art?"

One of the key categories of Western canonical aesthetics is the sublime, which plays a central role in the mechanism of catharsis. Immanuel Kant's *The Critique of Judgment* (1951 [1790]) presents a classical theorizing of this process, which stresses such outcomes of successful subliminal experience as regaining one's dignity; setting one's mind and imagination free; and sending a person through a purgatory, which enables moral elevation and resistance to the forces of nature. In the case of the decolonial sublime, Kantian nature is replaced by modernity/coloniality and our belonging to it in various capacities—from objects to subjects, from critics to accomplices and those who delink from it. Global coloniality is then illuminated in an image or a metaphor, momentarily lighting up the trajectory of further epistemic, ethical, aesthetic, and existential solidarity in subversion.

The cathartic mechanism is grounded in demonstrating the darker side of modernity—that of violence, injustice, the dehumanization of the large groups of people, the objectification of nature, and the delocalization of historically and culturally bound experience. Decolonial sublime acts through parody, irony, canonical counterdiscourse, deliberate and aestheticized nostalgia, grotesque, chiasmus, overlay. This sublime is not based on fear, as in the Kantian model, or pleasure linked with fear of the insignificant human being in front of the greatness of nature. Consequently, Kantian resistance to the forces of nature as an outcome of the sublime—and even Bruce Robbins's (2002) model of the sweatshop sublime as a realization of the global socioeconomic dimensions of being—are replaced with indignation, repentance, hope, solidarity, and, most important, resolutions to change the world to restore human dignity and the right to be oneself. The decolonial sublime dynamically combines the rational and the emotional in its constant multispatial hermeneutical effort (Tlostanova and Mignolo 2009), which requires active understanding instead of passive perception.

The decolonial sublime de-automatizes our perception to push us in the direction of agency—ethical, political, social, creative, epistemic, and existential. This leads to serious shifts in how we interpret the world and relate to other people. The decolonial sublime is grounded in overcoming in an existential or Zen Buddhist sense, in transcending in the Kantian sense, or, better yet, in transmodern delinking,[3] after which the artist and the audience need to relink with something or someone. Here, the negative resistance gives way to a positive re-existence. As essentially border thinkers and dwellers, decolonial artists delink from and relink with various Western and non-Western models, whereas the temporal dimension of such art negates any progressive unidirectionality and opts for the simultaneity of many times and spaces instead.

CHAPTER TWO

Decolonial Aesthesis and Post-Soviet Art

The post-Soviet subject is no doubt a theoretical construct whose validity is always threatened by its extreme heterogeneity. Yet there are certain social, political, cultural, and aesthetic factors that not only bind us all together, even after twenty-five years of the post-Soviet experience, but also make us occupy a particular nonspace in contemporary global coloniality and often trigger decolonial aesthetic drives among post-Soviet artists and thinkers. The affective sphere remains one of the very few areas left for the construction of a positive identity. The specificity of decolonial drives in the post-Soviet space is connected with their local histories and configurations of imperial difference. As a result, those locales that claim a (secondary and precarious) European belonging, at first demonstrate a catching-up complex and a longing to finally assimilate and become one with the old Europe (Kalnačs 2016a, 2016b). Later, many of them become disillusioned and turn to discursive and representational self-postcolonization and self-subalternization that, in its turn in some cases, develops into a decolonial sensibility (Jirgens 2006; Kovačević 2008).

In clearly non-European locales such as Central Asia and the Caucasus, decolonial drives are coded through postcolonial symbolism that is still marked by a difference between the Second World and the Third World. In a neoimperial space of Russia the appropriation of decolonial discourse takes its most dangerous form today: it is an imperial Soviet self-affirmation at the expense of blackening the stronger imperial rivals and racially stigmatizing the entire former colonial others—its own and someone else's. In the center of this configuration stands an ethnic Russian who practices white supremacy in front of any non-Europeans, and resents being rejected by the Western society which does not see him as part of its racial sameness. It is not surprising that Russian propaganda has offered one of the most malevolent and reactionary interpretations of the European refugee crisis (Shimov 2016). The recurrent argument was that Europe should let in and venerate the civilized white Christian migrants (i.e., racialized post-Soviet groups) instead of the "Muslim savages." Often this discourse interlocks with National Bolshevism and its aftermath or balances on the verge of openly fascist, ultra-right ideology.[1] The projection of decolonial arguments onto the racially same poor and disenfranchised others in contemporary Russia often takes the form of juxtaposing the provincial regions as colonized territories with Moscow as the evil metropolis sucking the blood out of its own citizens. The darker side of this appropriation of the decolonial discourse is xenophobia and chauvinism. It is yet another erasing of the problems of real (post)colonial others. This is a dangerous development for decolonial option: the very ease with which the most radical reactionary forces appropriate its ideas—from National Bolshevism (which today quickly turns into a glamorous form of fascism) to Alexander Dugin's neo-Eurasianist imperialism[2]—leaves a door open for the most negative scenarios that, unfortunately, can easily come true in Russia. The decolonial option can be used and abused by such problematic forces as easily as it is appropriated by grassroots initiatives and social movements. One of the interesting examples of such a creative yet problematic appropriation of decolonial discourse in contemporary Russia, which at times can slide into National Bolshevik discourse, is the Bombily Art Group, represented by Anton Nikolayev and Alexander Rossihin (Nikolayev 2011).

Bombily and the Decolonial Option

The strange name of the group evokes the image of the bombers in a literal sense. Yet it can also be translated into English as "cabbies" meaning illegal cab drivers with no license. This name is connected with one of the occupations of its members that not only brought them additional means of survival but, more important, allowed them to meet and speak with various passengers and discuss the social and political problems of contemporary Russia during the ride. This group's style, aptly called "Moscow Infantilism" (Parshikov 2008), is pointedly opposed to any conceptual and purely intellectual art that tends to be far from reality and the common people in the street. In most of its actions, the Bombily Art Group attempts to find ways back to the common people and elaborates a specific language that appeals to emotions rather than to the intellect. This is their way of decolonizing aesthesis.

One of Bombily's most interesting actions took place in May 2007, in collaboration with members of the internationally better-known group Voyna (War) (Epshtein 2012). It was called "White Line," and consisted in the symbolic cleaning of Russia by expelling the evil forces that have planted themselves in the city center and, according to the group's blog, "drawing the line between the righteous and unrighteous."[3] In spite of Bombily's infantile presentation the roots of this performance clearly went back to Nikolai Gogol's macabre novelette *Viy* (1835), in which the main character was fighting with the devil and his accomplices by drawing a white line around himself and reciting a Christian prayer. In Bombily's modern performance, the participants drew a white chalk line around the Moscow Garden Ring which traditionally divides the center of the city from its more democratic outskirts. Thus the activists encircled the evil zone and erected an invisible magical wall around it that went uninterrupted, despite highways, bridges, and underground paths.

Later Bombily projects included several car trips to provincial Russian towns, documented in road movies that attempt to reflect the differences between "Planet Moscow" and its many satellites living in different times and with different expectations for the future. Once again, the driving force was to try to break through and find a way of surviving for the ordinary human being in the outskirts of the former empire with no glamorous metropolitan symbols around and often with a clear realization of the doomed future. Several years ago, Anton Nikolayev, an art theorist, musician, activist, and member of the Bombily Art Group, became interested in the decolonial option. The imperial difference that Nikolayev obviously represents selects for itself certain parts of decolonial discourse that can be problematic, because it shows the possible darker side of the decolonial option when and if it is reinterpreted through the imperial difference. It then slides toward National Bolshevism, with its peculiar imperial revivalism grounded not in the idea of race or religion but rather some cultural, linguistic and broadly leftist egalitarian community that is initially color-blind as it is interested in coopting as many different people as possible into its ranks. But eventually this discourse can evolve into radical nationalism and fascism. It was not by chance that Nikolayev publicly joined Limonov's National Bolshevik Party after it was banned in Russia. In this gesture there was as much politics as actionist protest aesthetics.

In a recent conversation with Nikolayev, I told him that I was very surprised by his ardent interest in the decolonial option because I more often find like-minded people among racialized and colonized groups or artists. I wanted to understand what initially attracted him to decoloniality and what elements of decolonial thought he found relevant. Nikolayev pointed out that, in his view, post-Soviet Russia resembles a number of Latin American countries that over the past few decades have shaped their own, specific political discourse. He admitted that certain features of decolonial thinking such as theology of liberation or decolonization might seem to be exotic. Yet it occurred to him that something similar could emerge in Russia by analogy. The most attractive feature of decolonial discourse for Nikolayev is its optional nature (Mignolo, Escobar 2009), the fact that it does not require a strict adherence and does not attempt to replace all previous and existing discourses, but offers an alternative (option) that one can freely choose:

> The optional discourse of decolonization sounds like something that the minorities should speak, the autonomous regions and the home-rule local communities. In other words, I became interested in decoloniality in a political-technological way. I see it as a possible theoretical basis for a social technology that would be accessible and tactically convenient for the most microscopic agents of civil society. This is the most important element of decolonial discourse that I found not only interesting but also practically useful in its optionality. Also, as an artist and a critic I was interested in the concept of

aesthesis, which works well for the description of process-based and network art.[4]

To me it seems that there are certain aspects of Nikolayev's works which can indeed be interpreted in a decolonial way. Mainly it refers to the radical artistic reflection and actionism linked to the dichotomy of the city and the province and the embodiment of certain centrifugal tendencies that are becoming quite palpable today. For instance, he has made a series of road movies in many Russian provincial towns and has contributed a lot to the development of artist-in-residence programs at the Guslitsa art center outside Moscow.[5] It is therefore tempting to compare the boundary between Moscow and provincial Russia to the divide between metropolis and colony and hence label this as some kind of internal colonization.

Nikolayev reacted to this idea through criticizing the federalist political model. He opposed it to the strong local self-rule lamenting that, according to the Russian Constitution, local governments are not part of the official organs of power and are in fact, exiled to the civil sphere which is closer to the society than any public policy. The activist stated: "Decolonization seems to me precisely an attempt at bridging the people and the local government. At the same time, starting from the hypothesis that local governments in Russia could develop thanks, among other things, to independent network structures, it turns out, quite unexpectedly, that federalism is a serious rival to any local self-rule that has not yet elaborated its own language. In other words, there could be a competition between federalism and decolonization, and this is quite possible in the political-technological sense."[6]

In contrast with other theorists' views on the fundamentalist backlash, for Nikolayev the present-day Russian duality and division is structured around the ruthless competition of the two projects—the inertial progressivist Soviet one and the post–Pinochet rightist project, neither of which has yet been properly conceptualized. He believes that the Latin American experience of both options, which have already played out in many different ways and more than once, could provide valuable lessons for Russia as well, and particularly in the NGO sector and volunteer organizations, which are largely lacking the necessary conceptual instruments for their motivation.

I was also interested to learn if and how Nikolayev links the decolonial discourse with his own artivism and more widely with the radical activist art in Russia. It was crucial to understand how such radical activist art envisions its own future in an increasingly repressive society and how it assesses its chances to affect this society in any significant way. This is particularly important in Russia's changing political situation, when the artists are torn between state censorship and the necessity to become a commodity.

In this department Nikolayev's response demonstrated a much more mainstream artist's and critic's position than I expected. He pointed out the paradox of artivism: the more actions we take, the less art those actions can contain. He also linked art as such with the concept of newness and the "increment of knowledge," which betrays persistent and unconscious links to modernity. Nikolayev is aware of the traps of artivism such as becoming unfocused; losing aesthetic significance as it becomes a mere functional element of politics. Yet he is optimistic in his view of the actionist future:

> Actionism and other quasi-theatrical genres share a wonderful quality: they are able to resurrect themselves approximately every ten years. Societies can seriously change their highlights in such a time span, and it makes sense again to stage the provoking events, and receive a different specter of reactions. However, when the restricted tools of actionism are quickly played out, actionism, somehow, leaves the zone of art and becomes something strictly applied and escaping any positive aesthetic criteria. Representation remains a difficult theoretical problem for contemporary art. There is hope that the temporal extension of art, and the shift from object to process and to networking, allow an escape from conservative representational frames and alleviate the repressive impact of the system. But it is not yet clear how true and how important this is.[7]

While speaking with Nikolayev I also had a feeling that due to his much younger age than most of my other respondents, he did not remember the Soviet Socialist context other than through his understandably idealizing childhood experience. There was an obvious generation gap between those who suffered from repression and censorship and those who nurtured various forms of Soviet nostalgia. In reaction to my question on his attitude toward Soviet and post-Soviet sensibilities, he said, confirming my suspicion,

> I believe that the Soviet project was better than all others because I feel close to it and we can all be reflected in it as in a mirror. I am attracted by the progressivist part of the Soviet project; by its promise of the revolutionary renewal of the world. Also the Soviet attitude

toward science and education was good. Moreover, the Soviet system is attractive because of its ideology of the social state and its efforts to reach everyone. There are a lot of negative sides, as well. The USSR is our mirror and our matrix, which we are bound to continue reflecting on for centuries. The question is not whether we should discard or keep the Soviet legacy—it is impossible to discard one's own history, after all—but how we will finally reassemble it all. That is why local self-government and its connections with decolonization seem important for this matrix recomposition to be maximally profound.[8]

Multiplying Differences, or The Colonial Difference of the Imperial Difference

In this section, I analyze tendencies toward decolonialization in post-Soviet art by concentrating exclusively on those groups and people who share the postcolonial and post-Soviet predicament and who were, and are, "others" in the modern/colonial designs—Czarist, Soviet, national(ist) post-Soviet, and neoliberal global.

Postcolonial post-Soviet subjects experience a specific form of double-consciousness. In the USSR it was connected with a division between Soviet and national cultures, which sometimes merged in boutique multiculturalist forms, such as when official aesthetics prescribed how a national/ethnic author or artist should write or paint. Today the situation is even more paradoxical. There is a new official and safe norm adapted for the national art as opposed to unofficial critical art. The latter may be national in its spirit, but in its own dynamic forms, which are often far from any frozen and completely constructed authenticity. This is threatening to the post-Soviet nation-states, but also sells well in the West. As a result any serious and critical artist-activists (artivists) end up in yet another dead end, between the devil of the state and the deep blue sea of the market.

Post-Soviet postcolonial artists then experience an unpleasant déjà vu that, in some cases may lead to a development of decolonial sensibility. In the Soviet system artists had an uneasy choice between the Eurocentric academic education and their consent to play the role of craftsmen, reproducing the presumably age-old traditions in a restricted area of the so-called national/ethnic arts. In colleges and universities, the national departments of art, language and literature, dance, and music were always considered nonprestigious and therefore were easier to enroll. On the surface, this looked like a celebration of Soviet affirmative action, but in reality this structure strangled any real development of national/ethnic cultures in the colonies except in the Soviet package of the national in its form and socialist in its essence.

The students of these national departments were not taught any theoretical disciplines, and even the obligatory survey courses in the history of art, literature, or music, in their case were considerably shortened and simplified. From the very start then a hierarchy was established, within which it was taken for granted that artists do not need to know Renoir if they are going to paint *pahta* (cotton flower) ornaments on *piyālas* (traditional central Asian cups in the form of small bowls mostly used for serving tea) for the rest of their lives; musicians do not need to know Mozart if they are going to play *zurna* (traditional woodwind instrument similar to oboe, known in many countries of Central Eurasia) for the next fifty years; and poets do not need to know Shakespeare if they are going to recycle traditional oral poetic forms imbuing them with Socialist contents (e.g., by eulogizing collective farms and Lenin instead of national heroes and warriors). One can naively interpret this positively and say that if Mozart and Shakespeare symbolize Eurocentric values, then the indigenous people and the colonized groups may have been better off in Soviet academic institutions, since they were not asked or offered to study the Western tradition. Yet this was also a cunning form of coloniality, whereas the real way out should have been letting the young artists study both models, without constructing hierarchies.

At the same time, the interpretation of ethnic-national culture in this case was reduced to a set of simple devices that presumably could be applied to any content, including the ideologically Soviet one. Thus the study of native culture, art, or cosmology was limited to training the future artists how to use these devices, whereas the axiological grounds behind indigenous art were wiped off or made invisible. Luckily, this Soviet requirement was not followed too strictly and the colonies still had many masters, who continued to teach their pupils how to be in the world, and not just how to paint a pretty cotton flower on tea bowls. Certainly the restored and maintained accent on cosmological links between art and knowledge, art and the existential sphere, and art and contemporary life, instead of a purely instrumental understanding of art as a frozen repetitive device, had to be hidden to avoid Soviet repression. And it took many efforts by both the masters and their pupils to reconnect the native cosmology as a living entity and their everyday lives, in which any ethnic culture was always effectively limited to be represented just as a decoration (Abbasov 2005).[9] The artists could practice resistance only mentally or in indirect ways because any art that stepped outside the Soviet multiculturalist model immediately landed its creators in prison as bourgeois nationalists.

If one chose classical academic education in the art and the humanities, one had to reject all native ethnic-national elements and become homogeneously Soviet (that is Western and Russian in terms of aesthetics, and Socialist in terms of ideology). Yet since these artists were still not Russian (or Western) by origin, they had to know their place and be forever confined to a secondary status—for instance, to be good imitators of the "great" Russian/Soviet Socialist realists. There was no possibility for combining the consciously selected Western techniques and some national-ethnic aesthetic identifications. This was a weird Soviet/colonial form of double consciousness. One could expect that after the collapse of the Soviet system the ethnic-national art, music, and literature finally had a chance to develop their own forms rather than continue to be imitations of the Western or Russian originals or prescribed multiculturalist oeuvres. However the long awaited renaissance of indigenous art never really happened. The national continued to exist in its decorative forms. They just got rid of the collective farms and Lenin and replaced these recurrent images with artificially invented ancient traditions that were convenient for the new old elites. In the end there was another void. Any links with ethnic-national art forms, cosmologies and axiologies were irreparably destroyed. And this was one of the most appalling successes of the Soviet époque.

And yet there are still artists who manage to critically and dynamically engage with their national-ethnic elements, and Western and Russian canons, as well as with different subversive traditions within them. They try to remake and problematize all of these elements in their works. These impulses are decidedly decolonial, as the artists criticize both global modernity/coloniality and provincial local color from their border position. It is this kind of disobeying and delinking trickster artist that the repressive neocolonial and neoimperial post-Soviet regimes dread most. The return of repressive, and often fundamentalist, national and religious communities of sense today is often regarded as an echo of the Soviet époque; consequently, protests against this new-old repression often take the form of revisiting the dissident anti-Soviet past.

Post-Soviet artists coming from or connected with traditionally Muslim regions often reconstruct and deconstruct the Islamic sides of their

identities in decolonial ways fully understanding both the constraining nature of global modernity/coloniality, and the strangling power of any religious fundamentalism. These people do not simply go back to Islam after
the decades of the forced secular Russian/Soviet modernity. Rather, they
are looking at the Muslim symbols and signs through the critical lens of
modernity/coloniality without taking sides, and constantly negotiating their
creolized bordering forms of secular Western/Russian (post-Soviet) and
native/Muslim sensibilities. In the 1990s, artists from the Caucasus and
Central Asia, tired of the old socialist in essence and national/ethnic in
form formula, turned to various neo-mythological forms of representation
by means of recurrent leitmotivs and symbols such as dung, felt, trains,
heroes, and the Silk Road (Gamzatova 2009). This can be seen as part of a
wider phenomenon of ethnic renaissance that started in the Soviet Union
in the 1970s–80s and contributed to its demise from within. The 2000s
brought global and local social and political reality back into the art in Central Asia and the Caucasus. Many works attempted to re-create a dynamic,
if contradictory, dialogue between cosmological roots and contemporary
conditions, between local histories and global designs, in the destinies of
those who belong to the underside of modernity. This art can be called
"postethnic" in the sense that it strives to critically revisit and overcome
many recurrent elements of the ethnic art of the 1990s, contemplating
these elements through the prism of contemporary global and local social
and political concerns.

Decolonial Art in Central Asia?

A telling example of decolonial art in Central Asia can be found in the
openly repressive country of Uzbekistan, which combines some elements
of Soviet-style discipline and punishment with post-Soviet, statist, ethnic
clan lawlessness. Contemporary artists who criticize both Soviet and post-
Soviet national forms of unfreedom, and are aware of the traps of neoliberal globalization, are vulnerable in this environment. Post-Soviet artists
are exposed to the pressure of commercialization and commodification
of their works and identities. But they are also not free from state-induced
ideological censorship. This is the situation in which the Uzbek artist, philosopher, poet, and cinematographer Vyacheslav Akhunov now finds himself.
Forbidden to leave Uzbekistan (which continues to use the Soviet system of
exit visas, and his is repeatedly denied), he has had to limit himself to hold-
ing low-key "apartment exhibitions" in his home country while his works

travel the world. A number of important museums and private collectors have bought his art in the past two decades, and Akhunov has won several important prizes at biennials and festivals. But in most cases he is not even allowed to visit his own exhibition or collect the prize. This is the double existence per se, which makes Akhunov's life uncomfortable yet imbues him with an additional perspective. This would be impossible, had he been more integrated into the simulacrum of the local artistic world or had he simply been a Western artist belonging to the sphere of sameness.

Blind Alley (2007), one of Akhunov's most powerful video artworks, captures a peculiar post-Soviet despair that is echoed in works from several other post-socialist countries (e.g., in the Romanian artist Ciprian Mureşan's work *Leap into the Void, after Three Seconds* [2004]). Like many other examples of Akhunov's video art, *Blind Alley* was filmed in Tashkent's old city, where the artist resides. Several protagonists wander in the narrow, curved streets looking for a way out and always ending up in a blind alley as a pervading symbol of contemporary Uzbek life.

Akhunov plays on various myths, utilized by the new/old elites both in Russia and in Uzbekistan, placing them against the looming background of the global coloniality, intermeshing the imperial/colonial past and the neo-imperial/colonial present. Such is his series of collages based on counter-discursive interpretations of the nineteenth-century Russian painter Vassily Vereshchagin's militaristic Orientalist works. It includes *The Doors of the New Tamerlane* (2005), in which one of the guards from Vereshchagin's painting is replaced with a modern uniformed Uzbek security officer. Akhunov thus accentuates the immutability of a hierarchical power system that is hostile to its subalterns and the contemporary revival of the Timurid myth.

Another famous work by Vereshchagin that was reproduced in all Soviet history textbooks and is still proudly exhibited at the Tretyakov Gallery in Moscow is *The Apotheosis of War* (1871). With its stereotypical heap of human skulls, it is often interpreted as the artist's antimilitaristic statement. In Akhunov's version, the skulls are intact, but the surrounding desert is adorned with large advertisements for Coca-Cola and other staples of popular culture and signs of belonging to global modernity: a "peaceful" consumerist conquest still leaves human skulls behind while the present military leaders and dictators can be successful capitalists, building their fortunes at the expense of the former owners of these skulls.

The last painting in this series, *Return of the Forgotten Regiment*, reflects on the Russian/Soviet empire's relation to its former soldiers, and generally to all citizens. It originates from Vereshchagin's *At the Fortress Walls: Let Them Enter!* (1871), a painting that celebrates the Russian Army's "courageous attack" on Samarkand, in which Vereshchagin himself took an active part. Akhunov makes an almost imperceptible but powerful replacement: instead of the ruined Samarkand fortress wall, the regiment assaults a crumbling Kremlin wall that turns out to be made of clay. Symbolically, the forgotten regiment is paying back to the empire and taking revenge against those in power who sacrificed the soldiers' lives and then chose to abandon the former loyal servants to perish in the ruins of empire.

What Does It Mean to Be "Kazakhian"?

Previously nomadic Kazakhstan, which was flooded with millions of Slavic colonists in the Soviet years who successfully diluted the local population and made today's Kazakhstanian idea of nation a highly constructed one, is an interesting case of emerging decolonial sensibilities. Some of them take deliberately actionist forms, when artists exploit their over-exaggerated Asiatic features, making fun of demonizing Orientalist ideologies, still widely spread both in the West, in Russia, and in Central Asia itself. Thus, Said Atabekov has worked on peculiar assemblages that fused and superimposed presumably "traditional" and eternal ethnic-national features with bits and pieces of contemporary reality—often disturbing, threatening, and violent. However, these intrusions of modernity/coloniality into his characters' lives are invariably made nonaggressive, softened and domesticated to show that life goes on and easily swallows and reworks any alien elements, incorporating them into its system. In fact, it is the opposite of the usual assimilation and appropriation of colonial others through which the artist draws the attention to what was marginalized before.

Atabekov's decolonial counter-discourse can be exemplified by his most well-known and controversial work, *The Son of the East* (1995). He discovers an unexpected complex visual symbolism in *shanyrak*—a wooden ring with a cross inside, used to hold together the frame of the yurt (traditional Kazakh movable tent-house[10] By placing the naked figure of a teenage boy on the cross, Atabekov combines the post-dependence national symbol of Kazakhstan with the Christian imagery of crucifixion. At another important layer of visual symbolism, the image of the teenage boy mocks the ideal proportions of Leonardo da Vinci's Vitruvian man. In both contexts, the humanity of the protagonist is negated as he is made into an empty symbol of national or universalist humanist ideology.

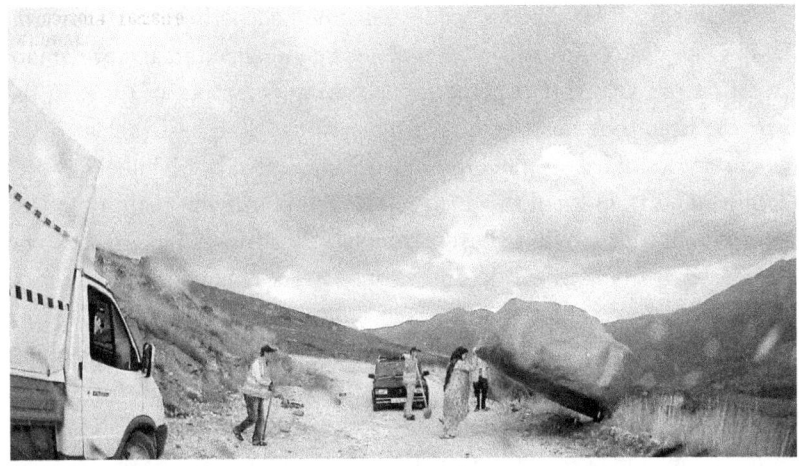

FIG. 2.1 Taus Makhacheva, *Super Taus (Untitled 1)*. Dagestan, 2014. Viral video, 2.16, color, sound. Courtesy of the artist.

In Atabekov's *Warrior's Cradle* (2007) and *Holy Family* (2001), the handle of the cradle is a Kalashnikov gun; instead of a canopy the family recycles an abandoned banner of the United Nations troops, while a group of Kazakh women in traditional clothes drags a faulty UN car through the steppe, using just a rope. This work somewhat rhymes with the Dagestani artist Taus Makhacheva's video artwork *Super Taus* (2014). Dressed in a traditional Avarian dress and headscarf, she is travelling in an old car along the unpaved mountain road, which is suddenly blocked by a huge stone. Three male workmen are unable to remove it to facilitate the traffic. The artist easily and nonchalantly does their job by herself, as many of her women relatives would actually do in their everyday lives. Such is her cunning play on the folkloric and mass cultural superheroes, merging with ordinary people from contemporary reality (Makhacheva 2015).

The Kazakh artist Yerbossyn Meldibekov's works combine postcolonial and post-socialist imagery and aesthetics, struggling to come to terms simultaneously with Western and global tendencies. Playing on his own demonized identity, Meldibekov revisits his Central Asian roots to transform himself into an Asian analogue of the paradigmatic barbarian. He becomes an Oriental other who has fallen out of time. His works are irreducible to the Western (and Russian/Soviet) canon, and to the so-called ethnic-national and ethnographic art. They are based on a creative, ironic and subversive reworking of all of these elements instead.

A number of Meldibekov's video-documented performances are unified by the dystopian space of Pastan as a generalized image of demonized Central Asia, that is perceived as having fallen out of time. In the name "Pastan" one hears echoes of the existing "Stans"—Uzbekistan, Afghanistan, Kazakhstan—but grotesquely exaggerated by Meldibekov's provocative and ironic stance, which rejects the prettifying tradition in the interpretation of ethnic culture and opts instead for a bloodthirsty and demonstrative type of exoticism. Many viewers in Russia and the West take this exoticism at face value, which allows them to rest peacefully with their reconfirmed Orientalist stereotypes, whereas Kazakh intellectuals often react indignantly, accusing the artist of unpatriotic gestures. Both groups remain blind to a significant gap between the artist's self and his often violent and bitter allegories of mute and dehumanized Central Asian subjectivity, devoid of any dignity or desire for freedom. Hence, the characters of Meldibekov's series are sold in the market like cabbage in sacks; live human heads stick out of piles of bricks or directly from the earth and are left to die slowly in the sun. Although Meldibekov defines "Pastan" as a message created out of disappointment with Gorbachev's and Yeltsin's reforms, its meaning is clearly more complex than the author's original intention (Fomenko 2013), as it embraces the leitmotif of essential powerlessness and dispensability of human lives, which overgrows the Central Asian local context in the direction of global social reality, where colonialism is being reborn as coloniality.

Meldibekov's *Gattamelata in the Hide of Genghis Khan* (2006) is based in a double critique of the Western canon and its neocolonial Central Asian incarnations, sharing the universal cult of militant authority and power. The artist criticizes both the pervasive self-Orientalization and derivative post-Soviet Eurocentrism of local Kazakh elites and superfluous and banal interpretations of national/ethnic culture. He accentuates the absence, the hiatus, and, ultimately, the unimportance of the military leader's actual identity—whether that leader is Gattamelata, Genghis Khan, or Tamerlane. This is expressed in Meldibekov's taxidermic tendencies. In *Gattamelata in the Hide of Genghis Khan*, as in many other works, he uses the preserved parts of dead animals' bodies—this time, a horse's legs with naturalistic physiological details of bones and veins. These legs also symbolize power and violence. The original "Gattamelata," from which Meldibekov copied his postcolonial caricature, was a statue of the condottiere Erasmo da Narni. It was erected in Padua, where Donatello immortalized him in the first Renaissance equestrian monument. This model was to be replicated in all the equestrian monuments thereafter—both in Europe and today in Central Asia as well. The capitals of Central Asian states have also acquired such monuments in the last twenty-five years. The "heroes" they depict are often obscure, or even completely invented historical personages brought back from oblivion. They carry no real significance for contemporary citizens of these nations. These nomads lack faces—or, rather, they are equipped with average Mongoloid features, resembling everyone and no one at the same time.

A similar misunderstanding on the part of Eurocentric critics takes place in the case of the Buryat artist Zorikto Dorzhiev, a cunning trickster who makes fun of unsuspecting audiences' assumptions that a savage from the Far Eastern steppe can make only simple objects with little aesthetic value. This artist regards the nomadic world of his contemplating characters not as much as a real physical material place, but as an infinite and flexible existential and metaphysical space, combining the personal and the cosmic. This decolonial Buddhist with a solid formal academic art education, which he soon rejected for being too Eurocentric, offers a virtuoso canonical counter-discourse of the most famous Western artworks, leaving no stone untouched in the department of classical aesthetics. Such is his *Gioconda Khatun* (2007), in which the standard of European beauty transmutes into a Buryat woman. Yet, a Caliban, painting an ironic Miranda's portrait to make her look like his mother Sycorax, can never be accepted into Prospero's reference system. A similar technique of repainting Western masterpieces, making their characters look decidedly Mongoloid and supplying them with Kazakh-sounding names, is used by Kuanysh Bazargaliev in his project *When Everyone Was Kazakhian* (2013).

The Kazakh woman artist Saule Suleimenova superimposes archival and contemporary photographs and painting in her multi-temporal and multi-spatial series *I Am Kazakh*. She carefully releases the forgotten and suppressed impulses and sensations of the beautiful, attempting to "reconnect and reconcile traditional Kazakh culture and the aesthetics of revolt, modernist artistic devices, the pathos of eternity, and the poetics of the everyday."[11] Suleimenova keeps coming back to persistent inferiority complexes, which are typical in contemporary Kazakhstan, where thinking and perception are still marked by coloniality: "Our people desperately want to look better. They are very much afraid that someone will think badly of them."[12] Suleimenova urges her compatriots to unlearn others' artificial ideas of the beautiful and sublime—Western and local—that were taught to

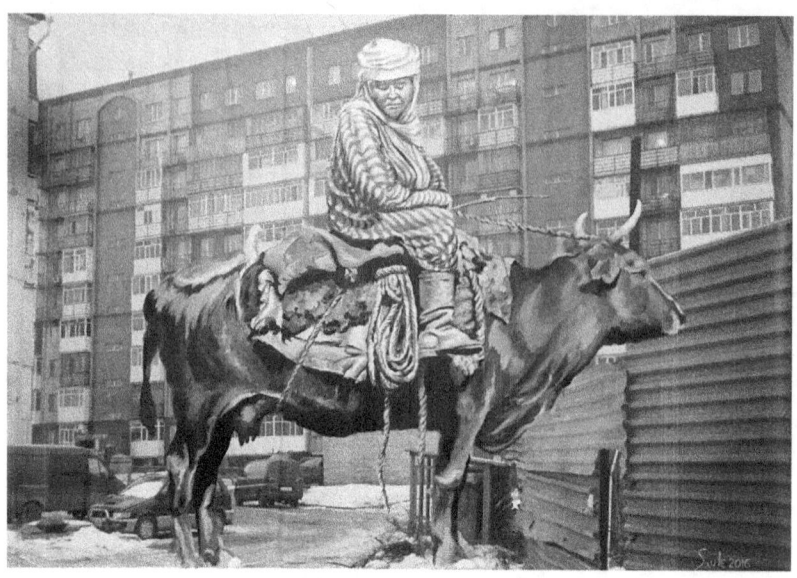

FIG. 2.2 Saule Suleimenova, *Cow Apa*. 2016. Acrylic in giclée print on canvas, 127 cm × 180 cm. From the series AstanaLine. Courtesy of the artist.

them as universal and natural. She is thus attempting to decolonize their idea of Kazakhness. Similarly to Meldibekov, Suleimenova was initially accused of taking an unpatriotic stance and disgracing the image of Kazakhstan in her works, which superimpose Kazakh faces from nineteenth-century photographs on the contemporary ragged walls of Almaty and rundown garages inscribed with endless advertisements. But this decolonial inoculation, shocking at first, is already producing results as more and more Kazakhs turn to Suleimenova's works as powerful aids for unconventional self-reflection and critical thinking at the crossroads of rationality and affect.

In *I am Kazakh* and in her recent series *Cellophane Painting*, where Suleimenova turns garbage (the used plastic bags) into art, she recreates a more complex and contradictory idea of reality than any official binary ideology is able to offer. She says that contemporary Kazakh reality is "awful and beautiful at once" (2010) and people must learn how to deal with it and how to appreciate this complexity, this symphonic nature of life. Art in its turn should not take this reality to flat and frozen images and stereotypes, to rosy prettiness or stylized archaism. In this respect *Cellophane Painting* is also a play on ethnic-national archetypes and stereotypes. The artist

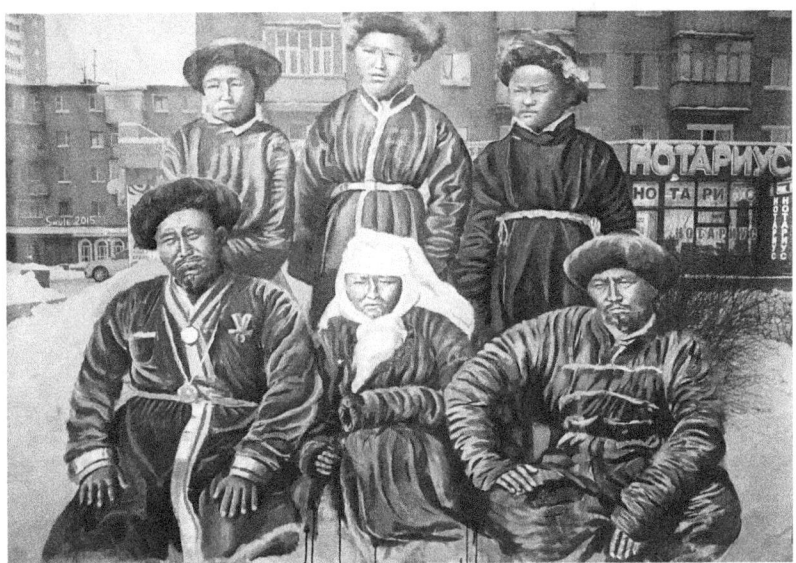

FIG. 2.3 Saule Suleimenova, *Notarial Office*. 2015. Acrylic on giclée print on canvas, 127 cm × 180 cm. From the series AstanaLine. Courtesy of the artist.

links them to a more global ecological dimension and a reflection on colonial forms of consumer society and second-rate modernity. The "paintings" in question are in reality made of recycled plastic bags of different colors. They often depict the primordial Kazakh steppe, which the staunch patriots venerate so much, yet continue to pollute with these very plastic bags, left over from their happy consumer purchases, to the point that the blooming steppe becomes invisible under the plastic garbage cover. Suleimenova does not avoid the overtly political themes either. Thus in *Zhanaozen* (2014) she presented the tabooed story of the massacre in the oil town Zhanaozen, when fourteen people protesting against the regime, were killed by the police on the country's Independence Day, and many were imprisoned (Ames 2011).

The Babylonian Caucasus and the Decolonial Aesthesis

Ethnic, linguistic, and religious diversity in the Caucasus, as well as the region's complex imperial-colonial histories, do not prevent it from keeping a pan-Caucasian community of sense and a shared decolonial subjectivity that is expressed in multiple forms in a number of works created by artists from the region. For instance, Azerbaijani authors problematize various kinds of modernities imposed on their open and changeable identity, always escaping any stiff prescribed forms. In his multilingual visual poetry, Babi Badalov mixes Latin and Cyrillic alphabets in an effort to make sense of his own diasporic queer existence in Europe. Orhan Guseynov's *Non-Standard* (2006) celebrates the fact that Azerbaijani culture refuses to fit into Western norms, even in such simple matters as sticking *chureks* (a kind of handmade cornbread) into an electric toaster. The Dagestani artist Magomed Dibirov's *soup* (2006) follows in this direction, showing the unhappy face of his niece as she refuses to eat a replica of Andy Warhol's mass-produced tomato soup.

Generally the Northern Caucasus artists are less openly decolonial as they still remain within the Russian Federation and must be more careful in their self-censorship and less open to any dialogues with European countries or much less with the Muslim world at large. Dibirov is a good example of such an Aesopian language. A native of Khasavyurt—a town at the border of Chechnya and Dagestan, the artist encrypts his political ideas in physically palpable material metaphors and often deliberately inanimate objects. Such a political still life is his *Member of the Federation*, where Russia is depicted as a brick wall in which one loose brick stands for Dagestan. Another example is *Temporary Truce*, featuring a meat grinder as an obvious symbol of power and a lonely tomato whose destiny is way too clear. In *Security Service*, Dibirov addresses Islamophobia through an expressive image of a beautiful arch, behind which lies the wonderful modern world and its guardian—a gigantic safety razor. The razor is awaiting the bearded Muslim protagonist (the beard here is a symbol of Muslim identity) as a necessary and inescapable condition of his integration into Western society.

"Super Taus" and Other Creatures

Another interesting example of emerging decolonial sensibility and aesthesis in the northern Caucasus can be found in Taus Makhacheva's performances, installations, and video art. One of the most successful young post-Soviet artists of non-Russian ethnic-national origins, Makhacheva has skyrocketed to international fame. She cannot be taken to represent merely Dagestani identity, yet at the same time she does not fit the neo-universalist globalist model favored by international contemporary art gurus. Makhacheva grew up in Moscow, earned her master's degree in London, and now divides her time among Dagestan, Moscow, and art residencies in Europe, Asia, and America. Yet this trajectory does not make her an altermodern artist à la Bourriaud. Her critical cosmopolitanism does not prevent her from maintaining strong links with the Caucasus. At the same time, she always keeps an ironic distance from this culture, to which she still partly feels she belongs. In this respect, Makhacheva often acts as a self-reflexive anthropologist-cum-artist, striving to better understand contemporary culture and the social and political reality of Dagestan, which is constantly torn between the modernizing and Westernizing tendencies, stylized Islamic models, pale remnants of the Soviet modernity, and persistent local indigenous traditions.

Even Makhacheva's earliest video works could be regarded as cases of decolonial aesthesis. For example, such was her performance *Carpet* (2006) in which she slowly wrapped and unwrapped herself into and out of a traditional carpet *kilim*, typical of Persia, the Middle East, Central Asia and the Caucasus. Her video is not exoticizing the carpets or celebrating carpet making as a traditional craft. Rather, it is a document of her struggling to come to terms and stay in touch with her own culture. Makhacheva performs this task through an extremely corporeal sensation, rediscovering traces of communal memory of other Caucasus women's bodies, wrapped and unwrapped into carpets to be kidnapped into forced marriages or sold into slavery. But in Makhacheva's case, wrapping herself into a carpet becomes a decolonial gesture of bodily reunification with the forgotten native sounds, smells, surfaces, textures, and tastes. The video recreates an almost palpable sense of the old rough carpet on the human skin. The artist relives these personal and collective embodied memories, using an old carpet as a decolonial tool, which is far from being a detached object of decorative applied arts, but rather acts as an almost living subject.

In the next decade, Makhacheva created several decolonial projects, including *Delinking* (2011), which interprets this concept in a peculiar body-graphic way. The artist wanted to embody the idea of delinking "from European thinking and ways of receiving knowledge, because in all cultures there are completely different systems for [and] practices of transmitting knowledge, cultural and intellectual evolution. [But] the world uses only the sanctified Western academic system" (Makhacheva 2011). In *Delinking*, Makhacheva's face is painted with Indian, African, and Middle Eastern ornaments. This kind of henna body art is used in various rituals on hands and legs but never on the face. As soon as her whole face was covered with ornaments, the spaces where the skin was still visible were filled with more henna, so that in the end her visage was totally covered with green mass.

After it got dry and was washed off, the face changed its color and became orange-brownish. It stayed so for about a week as a new mask, a new mocking identity, leaving a trace. The changing face color thus became a space for multi-spatial overlay of different cultural and epistemic systems.

Another decolonial gesture that emerges in several of Makhacheva's works refers to her play with space and spatial histories, which are always connected with bodies and embodiment. In *Gamsutl* (2012), she contemplates how human beings communicate with space, both natural and man-made, and with social and historical dimensions of spatiality through rediscovering and reliving in an utmost bodily sense, various forgotten and discarded spaces. The ruins of the abandoned village Gamsutl merge with the natural rocky landscape around. They imperceptibly blend with the cliffs, as the natural guardians, finally claiming this space back from the humans, who did not cope with making a livable and sustainable space on the top of the mountain. The performance centers on a ritual of remembering and reenactment of the spatial memory and embodied merging with this multilayered space, which witnessed the Russo-Caucasus War, Soviet modernity, and post-Soviet abandonment and return to nature. The protagonist of the video is a young man who is trying on various identities, imagines himself as a defender of Gamsutl, an assaulter, a warrior and citizen, and a brigade leader at a Soviet collective farm, merging traditional dance with symbols of Soviet modernity. Finally, he is just a human who is striving to understand what it means to be a tombstone, a watchtower, a crack in the dilapidated wall.

The close connections between spaces and bodies stand in the center of Makhacheva's attention in other works, as well. In *Landscape* (2013), she plays on the fact that, in the Avarian language, the word for "mountains" and "noses" is the same by presenting an installation of wooden copies of the real noses of Caucasus inhabitants, who traditionally are known for their large and prominent noses. She arranges the wooden copies in such a way that the installation becomes a replica of the Caucasus mountain range, made of the human noses, thus accentuating the bodily dimensions of the Avarian identity and humorously, their close connections with the environment.

A more openly political and disturbing dimension enters Makhacheva's experiments with space and corporeality in *Caspian Sea* (2014), first presented at the Uppsala Konstmuseum in Sweden. For the opening of the Friction Festival for performance art, Makhacheva prepared a geographical cake in the form of the real landscape around the Caspian Sea. She

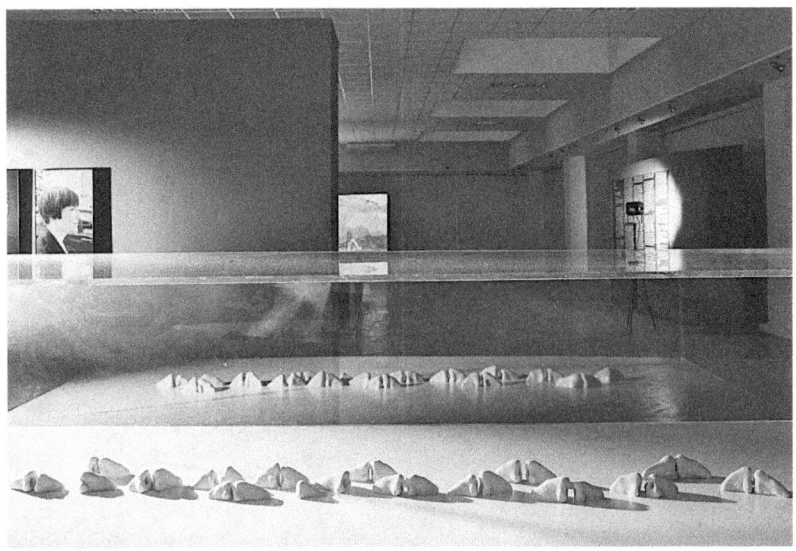

FIG. 2.4 Taus Makhacheva, *Landscape*. 2013–present. Series of objects, wood, dimensions variable. Courtesy of the artist.

was cutting the cake and distributing its pieces among the guests at the opening of the festival. The artist here literally embodied the metaphor of annexation as devouring and consuming countries and territories, which unfortunately is becoming a habitual practice once again. An obvious parallel to this gastronomic representation of aggressive geopolitics is the war in Ukraine. It is being distorted by propaganda of all the interested sides, which is also symbolically force-feeding the audiences with its indigestible dishes. An additional uneasy accent of this work is its historical parallelism. As in many other projects, Makhacheva first works with forgotten archival materials, which she studies at the State Documentary Archive in Krasnogorsk. There she discovered a documentary chronicle—one of the favorite Soviet genres of World War 2 period, in which a cake in the shape of the Caspian region was presented to Adolf Hitler by his generals. The artist is skeptical about the authenticity of this chronicle, as there is not a single episode where Hitler and the cake would share the same frame. But even if this were a montage, it does not negate the obvious parallel between recent geopolitical events and World War II history.

The most wide-scale expression of decolonial drives in Makhacheva's works is presented in her projects focusing on the decolonization of

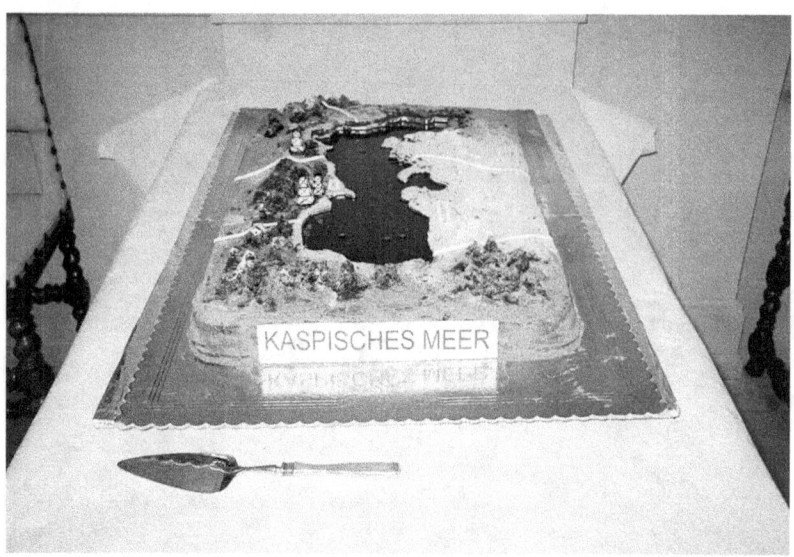

FIG. 2.5 Taus Makhacheva, *Caspian Sea*. 2014. Photo documentation of the performance *Cake*. Courtesy of the artist.

museums. This trend is gaining popularity all over the world, finding its realization in various museum interventions. They problematize the affective and conceptual operations, lying in the basis of the creation, appreciation and interaction with art and questioning the essentialist approaches, which were naturalized in the museum exhibitions before, through viewing "the established beliefs and institutions of our modern heritage as not only real but true, and not only true but good" (Curtis 2012, 74). These interventions are questioning the institutional framing of art and the linear progressivist narrative that museums continue to promote, thus problematizing the boundaries between representation and appropriation. As a result, a major epistemic and optical shift is enacted in a deliberate reversal of the roles of the audience and the objects it contemplates. Françoise Lionnet (2012, 192) cites the example of a Native American museum in which "exhibitions have been designed and controlled by those whose culture is on display. . . . Then the objects appear to be observing the spectators who become objectified by the masks whose eyes seem to be following their movements. In this case the exhibition builds a flexible, dynamic relationship with the culture it seeks to represent, and at the same time—with the viewer—neither of whom is entombed or simply reflected but put into a problematic dialogue instead." The exhibition "A Museum Looks at Itself," at the Parrish Art Museum in Southampton, New York in 1992, provided another interesting example of a critical, self-reflexive approach problematizing the imperialist and racist ideologies in the basis of this museum's principles of representation and selection.

Decolonial artists combine the roles of artists and curators by critically engaging permanent collections, the spatial and temporal structures of existing museums, and the ways those museums stage their interaction with the audiences. Often, decolonization of the museum takes the form of hidden or camouflaged interventions, grounded in deliberately accentuating of the elements of "tradition" as seen through a certain critical perspective—for instance, by presenting artifacts of a nonmodern culture alongside conceptual video art or performances by contemporary authors who are connected with that culture. Widely known examples of decolonial museum interventions include Fred Wilson's site-specific installations "Mining the Museum" (Maryland Historical Society, 1993) and "The Museum: Mixed Metaphors" (Seattle Art Museum, 1993). Wilson (1993: 101) is "interested in bringing historical information to the aesthetic experience in order to reveal the imperialist reality of how museums obtain or interpret the objects they display. Doing so makes clear the complexity of things on display."

Makhacheva has also contributed to the decolonization of the museum in several of her recent projects. The disciplining role of the museum as an imperial or national institution that provides a single, legitimized historical or aesthetic truth in a popular form is problematized in her small-scale work *The Way of an Object* (2013), based on the collection of the Dagestan Museum of Fine Arts. In this work, the artist plays with a number of museum objects, putting them in unfamiliar contexts outside the museum, such as at the entrance to the State Puppet Theater, where this performance first took place. This peculiar delocalizing, or "de-museumizing," was done to give voices back to objects that have been mute; to represent talking museum objects acting as characters in a puppet theater play written specifically for this work. The characters are an Avarian salt box; a Kubachi wedding bracelet; and the painting *The Bird Gamayun* (1895), by Victor Vasnetsov. In their endless arguments, Makhacheva rethinks the idea of narrating multiple histories in relation to a museum exhibition.

Giving mute and muted objects the right, and ability, to speak again is one of the more widespread approaches in the decolonization of museums. Often the main focus shifts from the (material) collection to a narrative,

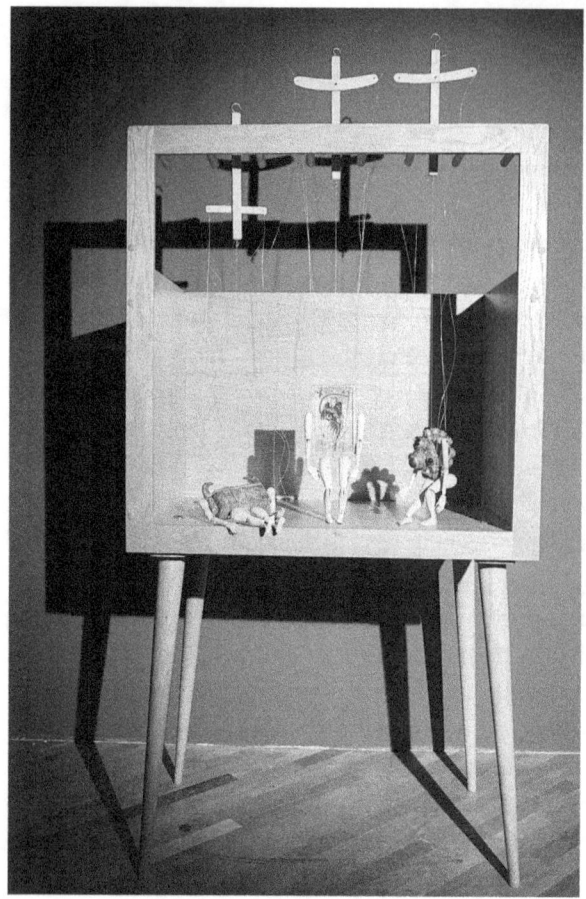

FIG. 2.6 Taus
Makhacheva, *The
Way of an Object*.
2013. Set of three
marionettes, mixed
media, dimensions
variable. Courtesy
of the artist.

which a curator builds around a set of objects—or in spite of them—or
even in the mode of objectless storytelling (Spalding 2002, 55). We find
something similar in *The Way of an Object*: when placed in a traditional
museum, the artifacts of Dagestani culture are torn from their context and
divorced from their sociocultural, utilitarian, and cosmological functions
and abilities. Vasnetsov's painting is also taken out of its original milieu and
becomes a dead representation of someone else's impenetrable canon. *The
Bird Gamayun* was taken to Dagestan to educate the local people according
to Western/Russian aesthetic norms; it carries a colonialist agenda that is
verbalized in the painting's lines in Makhacheva's performance. The piece
is, in fact, a museum intervention that is taken out of the museum and
placed right in the street.

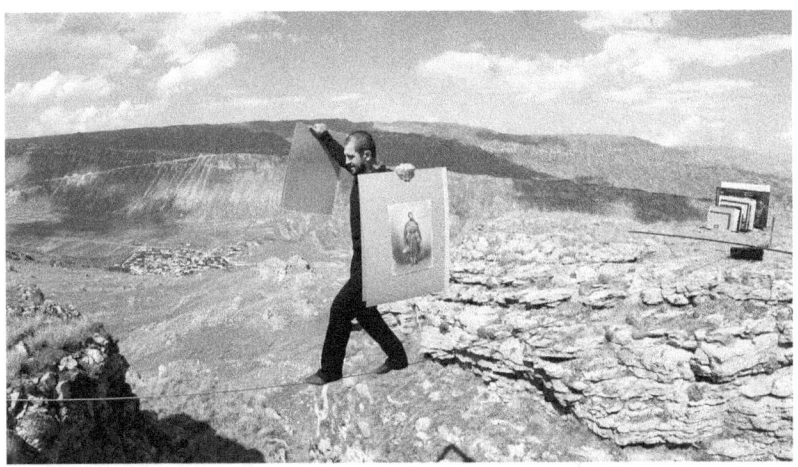

FIG. 2.7 Taus Makhacheva, *Tightrope*. Dagestan, 2015. 4Kvideo/73.03, color, sound. Courtesy of the artist.

Makhacheva has continued her decolonization of the museum and problematizing of art and artists in a more recent and larger project that combines performances and video art. At the Sixth Moscow Biennial of Contemporary Art in 2015, her work took the central place in the main pavilion and was presented in two forms: as an original videotaped performance called *Tightrope* (2015) and its Moscow version, which became a more ironic and metaphorical show titled *On the Importance of Pyramids, in the Cultural Perception, on the Strengthening of National Consciousness and the Shaping of the Moral and Ethical Landmarks*. The title rings a bell both with audiences who remember Soviet-style multiculturalism and with those who witness its new edition in the revival of moth-eaten imperial symbols and jargon. An important detail is that this performance was site-specific: it was staged at the heart of the Soviet VDNKh (Vystavka Dostizheniy Narodnogo Khozyaystva/Exhibition of Achievements of the National Economy) complex, which used to be the epitome of official multiculturalism and Soviet progressivism. This added ironic overtones of its own.

Like many of Makhacheva's works, *Tightrope* grew out of a concrete situation: the local museum of applied arts was provided with a better and larger building by the Dagestani government. However, the museum staff was asked to move all its collections in one day. Consequently the moving took dramatic and grotesque forms, when the ancient carpets were simply thrown out of the windows into the street to facilitate the moving process. People from the neighboring houses assumed that the museum was being closed and its collections were stolen or destroyed. But Makhacheva's work is ultimately not about the precariousness of museums as institutions and their difficult relations with power. The main metaphor used in this project—that of a tightrope walker taking the paintings, one by one from one mountain to another, evokes associations with the fragility of art as such in the face of the changing times, and also with human responsibility for preserving this art. Importantly, it is not just any art, but a history of Dagestani twentieth century painting and its complex relations with modernity. The artist contemplates the links and intersections between the so-called academic and traditional art, which used to be considered a mere craft before and at times even today.

It is significant that in *Tightrope*, the paintings, which are copies of the sixty-plus main works of Dagestani fine art, are carried across the abyss by the local master of tightrope walking Rasul Abakarov whose family has been rope walking for five generations. This is clearly not an academic, but an indigenous and popular kind of art, as in the case of the puppet theater in the previous project—a craft which has existed for centuries and is still alive. But Makhacheva goes further and gives the rope-walker a strange balance—the problematic canvases of Dagestani artists who, due to the Soviet modernization, were educated in the classical academic tradition and learned to paint in the Russian and Soviet (mostly realistic) style, thus fusing the ethnic-national subjects with essentially Western (though camouflaged as Soviet) aesthetic forms and norms. However the rope walker does not discard these obviously secondary and imitative works. He carries them carefully from one mountain to another. He is not a Caliban rejecting Prospero's education, then, but a balancing negotiator who is always on the edge, always at the border. This is also a fitting description of Makhacheva's work.

In *Tightrope* Makhacheva problematizes models of appreciating and transmitting the history of twentieth-century Dagestani painting and graphics, contemplating whether and how this art can become recognizable in a wider context. The video documentation of these performances was immediately acquired by the Van Abbemuseum in Eindhoven, The Netherlands, and Belgium's Museum van Hedendaagse Kunst Antwerpen (Antwerp Museum of Contemporary Art), for their permanent collections. And this is in itself a way of making Dagestani artists (both contemporary, like Taus Makhacheva, and the forgotten ones, the copies of whose work are carried across) visible and known in the world. Makhacheva draws our attention to how complex and unpredictable are both the creative process and its legitimation. She sees artists as taking a risk with every new project, just as a tightrope walker does with each new trip across the abyss. But she also reflects on the importance of the custodians and keepers of continuity, who are skillful acrobats, risking their lives for the art's sake. It is a musing on the complexity of the ways of transferring the ethnic-national cultural traditions and the precariousness of artists and their work. Its results are never known in advance—we cannot know if success or failure awaits us as creators, and many ingenious works never find their way into museums, collections, and cultural memory, figuratively falling into the abyss of oblivion.

The museum in Makhacheva's *Tightrope* is the opposite of the notorious white cube. It is rather presented through the two destination points linked by the rope. The first is a semblance of a bicycle parking-stand, in which the paintings are located so close to each other in the racks, that they are almost breathing in each other's backs. The second is a metal cage, in which the canvases have a little more space, as in a real museum storage. It manifests the idea of a movable museum, which has attracted Makhacheva for a long time. What I find liberating in this work is that art in its precarious and vulnerable situation of being balanced by a rope walker over the abyss, is paradoxically much more living, breathing and free, than when it is placed in the dusty halls of any traditional museum. At this point the paintings suddenly become part of the decanonized present, not yet or no more in the museum. This invigorating affective moment of reviving the art through a tight-rope walking experience, was reproduced at the Moscow Biennial, where instead of the missing real mountains Makhacheva constructed the imagined ones—the pyramids which were made out of the acrobats' bodies. The young athletes proceeded to do the same job as Abakarov did before— carefully, one by one they carried all the sixty one paintings from the bicycle stand to the metal storage on the other side of the hall.

A Caucasus Midnight Child

The Chechen Aslan Gaisumov is another example of a young artist from the Caucasus who has quickly gained international fame. Many of his works tell about the war, which has affected his life from its start, as Gaisumov spent his childhood in a refugee camp in Ingushetia. Yet he finds unusual and indirect ways to tell the war narratives, avoiding both sensationalism and the documentary dryness of official military reports. His view is never that of any fighting side; rather, it is of the ordinary people who find themselves in the

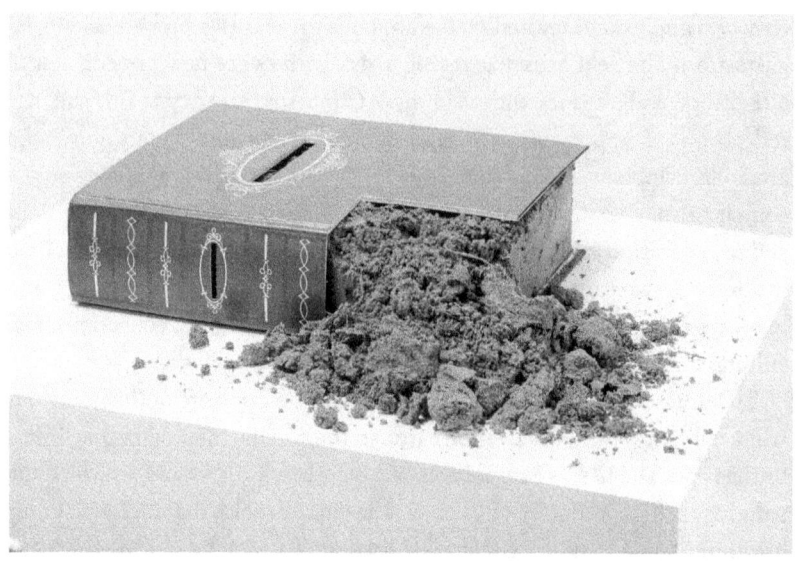

FIG. 2.8 Aslan Gaisumov, *No Need for Theories*. 2011. Mixed Media (book, soil), 7.5 cm × 12 cm × 26 cm. From the series *Untitled (War)*. Courtesy of the artist and Zink Gallery, Berlin.

midst of war against their will. One of his best-known works, the series *Untitled (War)* (2013), consists of books that all bear traces of war. The books act in unusual and unnatural functions. They are witnesses, victims, and even accomplices of the war crimes. The books may be used to make fires to warm up the children, but they may also contain clockwork bombs and be intended to kill and not to educate. In Gaisumov's works stark metaphors often reveal their scary real side—in this case, it is the books that normally represent everything that is opposed to war, such as human culture, intellect, knowledge, and poetry. Yet at the same time, the books are not just representations; they are real traces of human lives continuing in spite of the war.

The same shifting and liquid border between stark metaphor and cruel reality is at the center of Gaisumov's *Volga* (2015), which may look like a grotesque exaggeration of the penchant for extended families typical for the natives of the Caucasus and a play on the stereotypical Russian fear of these clans invading Moscow. If its characters were going to the market or just to visit relatives in the village, even were moving to Moscow in quest of a better life, the piece would have been merely a funny video of twenty-plus people slowly disappearing, in contradiction to all physical laws, into an old

Soviet Volga car. But the point of decolonial catharsis here is that it all really happened. When Grozny, the capital of Chechnya, was bombed by the Russian Army, Aslan's family first decided to hide in their native village in the mountains. To save as many people as possible, they really gathered and fit twenty-six relatives into a single Volga. Reflecting on this event today, Gaisumov realizes that the situation looks like a slapstick comedy. Yet it is tragic, as well, if we look at it from the time perspective of twenty years later and with an awareness of all of the ruined lives, deaths and losses, new beginnings and vanished hopes. The decolonial optic in this work hides precisely in this temporal lag, in the appreciation of what happened after the characters got into the Volga. Yet the video is not negative; it is full of humor and self-irony. It celebrates the peoples' ability to see the lighter and funnier side of any cheerless event—an ability that helps them to survive and prevail in any situation that is obviously the case of Chechnya and its long-suffering people.

Nevertheless, Gaisumov realizes that the cataclysms of recent history, the many layers of colonization, repression, destruction, exile, have been hard on the Chechen culture, making it at times almost impossible for it to survive. In a number of his works, the artist reflects on the ways of this survival in utmost situations, when completely different experiences and outlooks make generation gaps hard to breach. Each generation of Chechens has its own memory and its own version of history. Older people remember Stalin's deportations; the generation born immediately afterward, however, is free from that trauma and tends to idealize the Soviet Chechnya of the 1960s and 1970s. Gaisumov's peers grew up in tents and basements, hiding from the army's attacks and bombing; the younger generation of Chechens may not know what Grozny looked like before it was rebuilt by Ramzan Kadyrov as a shameless replica of the United Arab Emirates. What makes all these people Chechens, if anything? the artist seems to ask.

In fact, in one of our many long conversations over Skype, Gaisumov went even deeper, questioning the pervasive local patriotic pride of Grozny and thus moving to the previous layer of colonial history and problematizing the collective memory. What is Chechnya's capital, Grozny (lit., "fearsome" in Russian), after all, if not a military fort in the Caucasus redoubt line, built to "protect" invading tsarist Russian troops from the "attacks" of the unconquered local people and later made into the capital of one of the Soviet "autonomous" republics under total Russian control. Grozny was mostly reserved for the Russian/Soviet settler colonists; no locals were even allowed to live there until the last decades of the twentieth century.

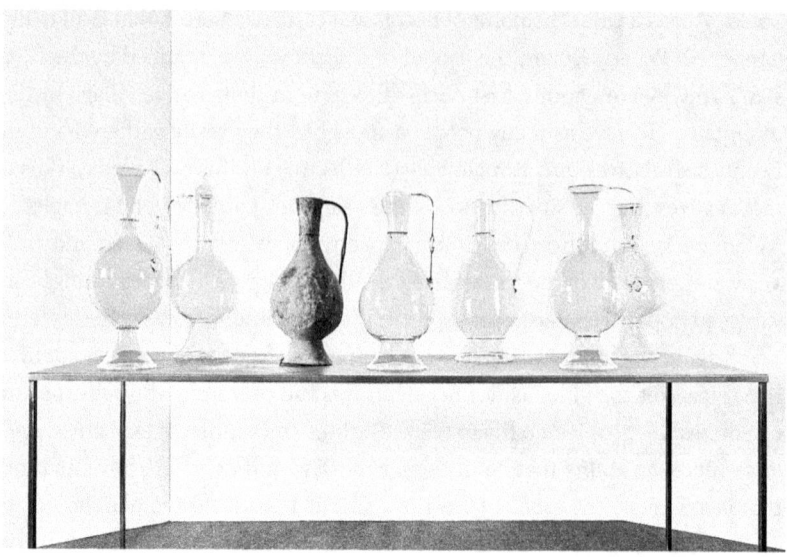

FIG. 2.9 Aslan Gaisumov, *Untitled*. 2015. Mixed media: one original Chechen water jug from the nineteenth century; six glass copies of the national Chechen water jugs. Courtesy of the artist and Zink Gallery, Berlin.

Gaisumov, like Makhacheva, acts as a participative anthropologist in dialogue with the audience's aesthesis, evoking bodily memories, sensuous responses, and erased and forgotten historical realities. In *Untitled* (2015), he uses Murano glass in the form of the traditional metal jugs women used to carry water in Chechen villages in the past—that is, when people were not thinking of only physical survival and were not forced into a permanent state of exception, making them forget about unimportant things such as the crafts and traditions that were slipping into oblivion. Gaisumov's jugs are made of the transparent Murano glass and are devoid of any utilitarian purposes. Rather, he offers an embodied vision of an ex-colonial ethnic culture. It is a reflection on temporality, on the whimsies and manipulations of memory and the difficulties of recovering the communal object in the world of commodities. Gaisumov strives to detect, in what elusive and escaping images, objects, memories and sensations a culture continues to live, when it is constantly uprooted, exiled, destroyed and remodeled. His jars are an attempt to represent such an embodied memory as the only remaining way of preserving the cultural constants for the future generations. The jars are transparent, clear and lucid structures, which can be later filled with any meaning by each new generation.

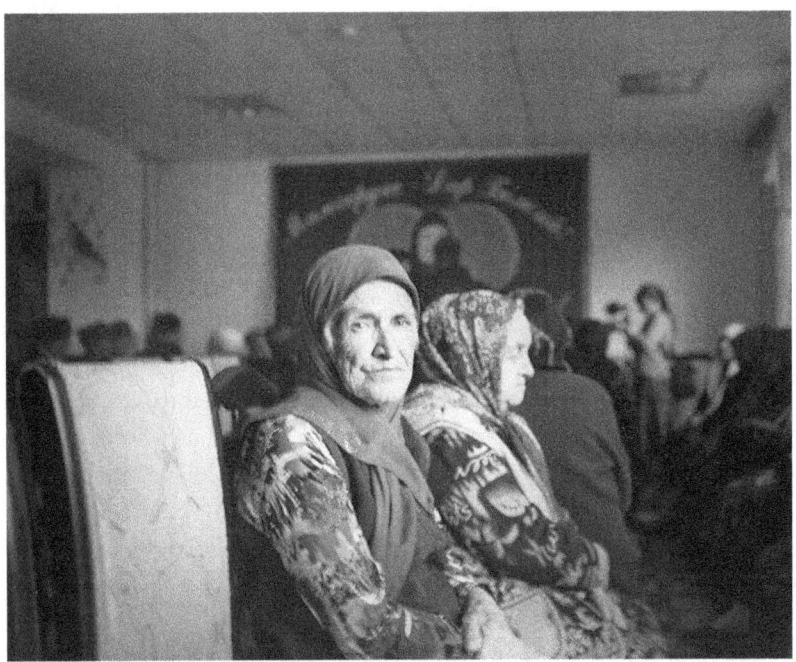

FIG. 2.10 Aslan Gaisumov, analogue black-and-white photograph for the project *People of No Consequence*. 2016. Courtesy of the artist.

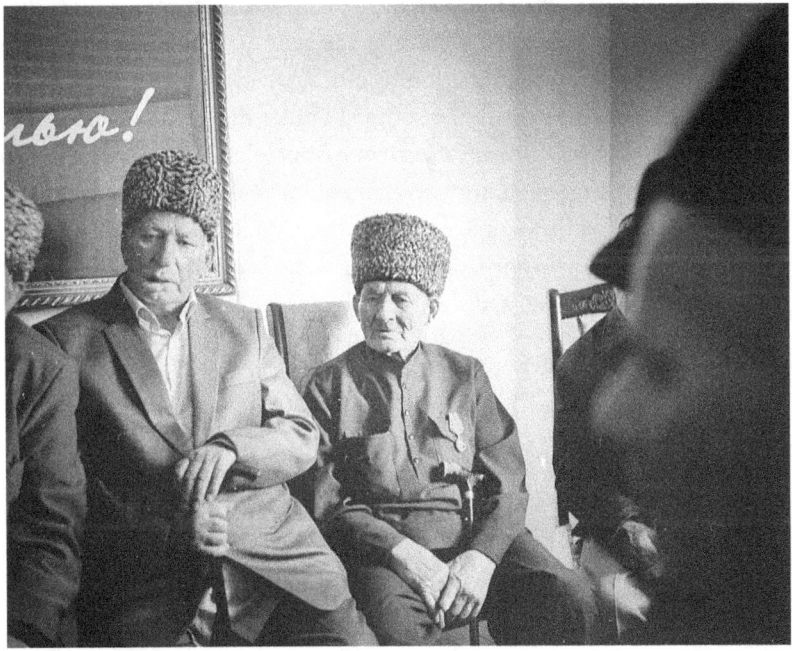

FIG. 2.11 Aslan Gaisumov, analogue black-and-white photograph for the project *People of No Consequence*. 2016. Courtesy of the artist.

Gaisumov believes that culture is not stagnant. It is not waiting for the return of its exiles, which makes us all potential strangers in our native lands. Any attempt to revive original traditions turns out to be false. Gaisumov explained to me that his idea to make the glass jugs was prompted by ancient vessels that are put together from remaining bits and pieces and then exhibited in museums. In many cases, the missing parts are replaced with glass elements. In the case of Chechen culture, almost everything is missing; therefore, making a metaphor of this culture as a glass jug is a powerful, if indirect, way to admit that the tradition is gone, that there are no authentic parts left. Today such jugs risk becoming dysfunctional objects that do not fit into any culture. There is no brook left to which women can go to get water. There are no people who can tell us who owned the jugs just by looking at their shapes and ornaments. The meaning of such actions has been lost forever. Yet, as in the case of *Volga*, Gaisumov does not see this as a tragedy. For him, a culture that is always on the road can find new forms of survival. The jugs are empty and waiting for new generations to fill them with their own meanings.

Decolonial aesthesis in the former Soviet Union acquires different, often unexpected forms that merge and juxtapose the postcolonial, post-socialist, global neoliberal, national fundamentalist, neo-imperial and several other dimensions. Yet in each of the analyzed cases, the artists try to put together a complex and multilayered picture of the post-Soviet human condition and reflect on the present and future of the people living in this world. They do this from the position of critical border detachment that allows for successful de-automatizing of aesthetic principles and is often linked to efforts to accentuate the suppressed elements of aesthesis. As a result, such works have broken through to a set of refreshing decolonial affects. This urge is carefully kept away from any dogmatic interpretations and seen instead as a flexible, live, and shifting field of social, cultural, artistic, and existential creativity.

CHAPTER THREE

A Woman Who Has Many Selves
and Takes Over Many Spaces:
A Conversation with Liina Siib

Liina Siib is one of the leading Estonian visual artists, feminist thinkers, curators and activists who represented Estonia at the 54th Venice Biennale with her photographic project *A Woman Takes Little Space*, exhibited at Palazzo Malipiero in 2011. Interviewing Liina was quite interesting for me as we belong to the same generation and also share the post-Soviet sensibility. The latter is true in spite of important differences in our experience and descent, in spite of the fact that, in my life, the postcolonial element prevails. Siib is connected with Estonia, which for many centuries has undergone a number of direct and indirect colonizations and assimilations, by both the more powerful Western European states and also the subaltern Russian empire and, later the USSR marked by the imperial difference. This shared Soviet experience still holds our common hermeneutical horizon together and allows for numerous critical conceptualizations and reflections.

The second node of our affective communication is feminist solidarity, which is also marked by the postsocialist condition. Positionalities such as Siib's are crucial for any efforts to conceptualize the nature of imperial difference and the paradoxical forms of colonial difference it generates in the cases

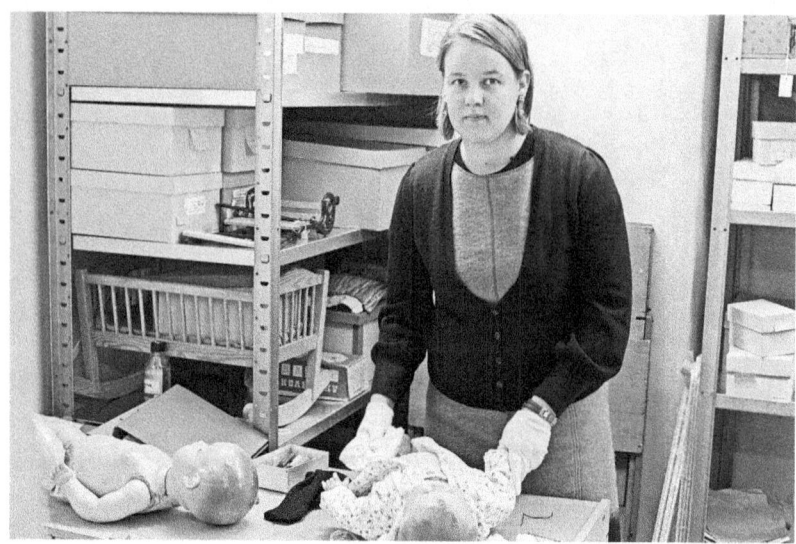

FIG. 3.1 Liina Siib, *A Woman Takes Little Space*. Ongoing series since 2007. Digitally edited analogue color photography, pigmented ink print, 30 cm × 45 cm. Courtesy of the artist.

when the "colonies" initially are more successful in their economic, social and cultural development than the metropolis. Today's belated and ultimately failed return of these countries to the European bosom has exposed the older and never properly critically assessed layers of the Baltic identity connected with internal European colonization and the forceful transformation into "second-rate" Europeans who are once again put into the state of dependence and forever catching up the neoliberal global modernity/coloniality.

MADINA TLOSTANOVA: Having seen several of your projects, I have an impression that space and spatial history are important categories in your work. I would like to ask you about your own perception of space (maybe in relation to time), home and "unhomeliness" to use Homi Bhabha's famous definition for " the condition of extra-territorial and cross-cultural initiations" (Bhabha 1994, 9); the spaces of freedom and constraint, space and/as corporality, especially gendered corporality, in the context of the East European postsocialist local history?

LIINA SIIB: It seems to be so. Indeed, I see and experience the world around me through places and spaces. Space can be perceived as a substance where all sorts of things can happen in which human beings are involved. It means how ordinary people act and operate in different spaces, ideologies and systems, how do they find mechanisms of resistance. What can we do with the space, indoors and outdoors, what space is left for women? Or what has come through the history of a place that has been intriguing, pointing at something relevant in the present, which could be rebuilt, restaged, reenacted, reinvented and represented. I have preferred urban spaces and the spaces with a dark history, execution sites, and some strange empty places in cities as "the scenes of the crimes," after Walter Benjamin, who was inspired by the images by Eugène Atget. The place can be fixed and indifferent, but a scene already presumes a participant, a distance, a viewer, the meaning that something can happen there or has already happened.

I agree to the most with Michel de Certeau that a space is a practiced place. A place that can be suitable for the performance, a place as a stage—it can become a space through directing its possible social agendas into mise-en-scènes and *tableaux vivants* depicting desirable ideologies and conversations. The possibility of a mise-en-scène turns these locations into hidden treasures, mining fields for artists or narrators. A spoken space is a space that has its stories where something that has happened will be revised and retold in a contemporary context. As de Certeau put it haunted places are the only ones in which people can live. Plus, if one happens to be a camera-based person, add the "optical unconscious," a term coined by Benjamin, so very true. Unspoken and invisible places. Haunting places and social spaces. Other spaces or heterotopias as Foucault described them. Thus, there are countless ways to practice space every day, in order to evoke one's fantasies and dreams, to call social ghosts back. It has been a pleasure to find out whether it is possible to examine the space through its representations. How the actual space becoming a representational space could make invisible social structures visible and present.

Places that still keep appearing in my dreams belong to my childhood—the flat where we lived—it was not very big but the outdoor space was a kingdom nearby the south border of Tallinn that contained a river, a forest, huge meadows, many children to play with, some strange characters which could be seen as "others"—drunkards, tramps, political abjects and persons with social stigmas (no one spoke publicly of those who returned from Gulag concentration camps), black marketers, Russian army troops and hippies among other remarkable figures. Our homely "Cold War" time. I guess this setting created a certain carnivalesque, enchanting fabric, a permanent strain for freedom whatever it means.

These oneiric places revolve around our small kitchen, the gas stove, the Snaigė fridge, the bathroom where my parents developed their black and white photographs in the weekends and the transistor radio where my mother listened to the Voice of America. I was sent to calm down in the dark bathroom or in the corner of the living room when I had been a naughty girl. Pedagogical spatial practice of introspection! To track down the genetic relationship to the space as much as I remember and have been told one of my grandmothers died young because she spent all her physical strength and efforts to create a huge fairytale-like flower garden by the farmhouse, the other grandmother who used to move around all of the furniture in her house every other month (alone! heavy early twentieth-century solid wood stuff), my mother who was keeping the places where she lived under a perfect structured control and order, just places and not people, but perhaps, who knows, keeping certain control over the family via her space, myself—ending up drifting in the streets and sometimes designing temporary furniture for exhibitions.

A nongendered flânerie. My first urban walks in Tallinn and Saint Petersburg in the 1980s as an art student, continued in 1992 in Paris, in 1995 in New York, in 1998 in San Francisco, in 2002–2005 in London, etc. Walking and walking and feeling the city in my feet, in my legs, in my head, waiting for a change in atmosphere in different neighborhoods, outskirts, wasteland, docks, warehouses, poorer suburbs. I usually do not feel much comfort in posh places, in the areas where money speaks. It is a too predictable setting. In Estonia I can go around and look for the metaphysics of spaces and buildings, in Beijing or in London, being more and more influenced by anthropology and sociology I wonder how people perform their everyday activities.

While walking I can compose texts in my mind, settle down and up ideas that circle in my head. It reminds me of a Kantian practice: he is told to have been going for a walk every day at a certain time in the main park of Königsberg. In 1999, when I happened to visit Kaliningrad, I decided to discover his possible tracks, but found only a miserable, wild and neglected place without any spell of aesthetics. In the Soviet period, we desperately wished to be part of the Western system, now we share its modes of production and democracy but we are still Eastern Europe. Maybe it hurt in the beginning, since we wanted nothing to do with the Soviet system and its traces. We knew the West as a representation, as the "langue," but we could not practice it as a "parole." It has been interesting to follow how one rhetoric is replaced by another, quasi-religious "new human" politics turns into an esoteric global consumer politics. Although we swim in the pool which is tiled with Western Paroles, this is not enough to overcome the psycho-geographies—whatever is the system, we are still not perceived by the West as part of it but rather seen as the postsocialist space. And who cares, except perhaps some politicians? One gets used to this particular identity. The most stunning thing to realize in transformations is that the systems can be transformed while the people can hardly do so. All that has been repressed returns at some point. The revolutionary spirit with its burning flames fades away fast, but its ashes become a great fertilizer for the spirit of conservatism and conformity.

TLOSTANOVA: Post-socialism is a problematic construct and yet it is a shared past, particularly for the people of our generation, a complex experience that we cannot undo as much as we wanted to. It is folded in our embodied memories, in our geopolitics of being, of gender, of perception. How do you feel about the postsocialist critical agenda in contemporary art and/or activism today? Is it viable and promising or doomed to be more and more ossified and "museumized"? We are all different of course, and yet is there anything that can allow us speaking of the "postsocialist subject" or maybe even "postsocialist woman" and if so, what lies at the core of this (self)identification? Virginia Woolf's famous concept of the room of one's own—how does it work in the case of the postsocialist women or does it at all? Can the shared Socialist experience be a source and a ground for a possible coalition to make our world a better place for us all?

SIIB: No, we cannot undo it. As I just explained, it is impossible, we embody it. Our bodies are trained under the Soviet discipline, in its kindergartens, its schools and universities, in the working places. As much as we wish to undo it, our bodies still remember it and act accordingly. Living in the Soviet Union was not my personal dream, but at least this bad dream ended in 1991. Its totalitarian regime had been violently imposed onto my country, Estonia, and it made systematical efforts to destroy the local spirit, memory, fabric and flesh. I do not know anyone who did not suffer from it. I think we still do. Even if the bodies survived, the souls are corrupted by the conformity to reality.

Since Socialism in Soviet understanding meant a totalitarian regime, it was a distorted version of Socialism. It meant double exploitation for women. It meant being placed in prison or mental hospital if one was not conformist enough. Maybe the best of this Soviet experience was that so many of us adopted an absurd relationship with life, an immunity to empty words, a prompt ability to detect lies, a skepticism of the state and any reforms, a tactic of resistance. The worst legacy of the Soviet Socialist system is perhaps the contaminated concepts of the left-wing ideas such as solidarity, unions, emancipation, equality, even the word "Socialism" itself was a taboo for some time.

Postsocialism as a construct could help us put the lived experiences into a critical context, to compare the Socialist conditions of the second half of the twentieth century with the present neoliberal agenda. The experience of living under the Soviet regime could be taken as an asset helping to realize what it means to live in a free world. What are these two systems about, where do they overlap, why do they go in opposite directions? What is still wrong in this picture?

Of course, some people whose roots are in the Soviet regime experience today a Stockholm syndrome and even long for the Soviet past (why?—"at least there were neither refugees nor homosexuals"). Others who are in power refuse to see any alternatives to their ruling methods which is obviously a manifestation of "the one party" syndrome. I think it is far too early to throw the postsocialist construct into the waste bin or place it into a museum.

In every evil, there is something good to be considered, in the Soviet Socialism maybe there were examples of social welfare, education and solidarity, at least in words. The capitalist abundance has helped to overcome the everyday lack of goods for many; it has brought freedom of speech and travel. But it has not obliterated poverty. The

Soviet trauma lies deep inside us beneath the new layers of life and affects us more than we would like to admit. This postsocialist space around us seems to be an aura and a stigma at the same time. Yet, it ought to be discussed through a contemporary prism, to see how we ended up where we are now. Was the Socialist condition the reason or something else? As our society is turning to conservative values in full speed, there is often a *déjà vu* feeling from the 1980s—the strange hollow rhetoric, the doublespeak, bureaucracy, the party system and the loyalty to the party, scheming, careerism, nostalgia for the Soviet period, intolerance of the other, living in the bubble, social blindness, corruption, etcetera.

Contemporary art can deal with these issues critically. It can provide strategies to question conformity and conservative values. Even more—art can help provide resistance to different policies of obedience. There is a problem that quite often these themes get labeled and ghettoed, and put aside because they are not considered to be the proper subject of contemporary art as an aesthetic concept. But I do not see anyone else to deal with these issues rather than contemporary artists who have time to tackle the whole picture in its entirety, and to carry on their artistic research of the social topics. How to maintain critical positions in contemporary art is more and more under question. How to make a work that is intellectually engaging? How to avoid the blindness of the social issues, how to give voice to different agendas in order to make them visible, even if these themes are not popular, entertaining, or presenting another model of success. Maybe Eastern Europe as a place with a weaker art gallery system is indeed the right space to make art from the critical position and to find time to consider the politics of representation? And please, never forget about the poetry when the personal becomes the political.

I played around the ideas from different systems and ideologies in my interactive performance *Mass Line*, produced by the Lilith Performance Studio in Malmö in the autumn of 2013. It was based on my notes from Beijing, China, with its communist Capitalism system and watching all the James Bond films, something that was banned in the Soviet Union until the 1990s. The performance merged China and the Western political ideologies through an analysis and practice-oriented observation of systems, prohibitions and orders, both large and small.

In the course of *Mass Line* that engaged around forty professional and amateur actors and the audience, we asked ourselves what space we can claim when there is not any. In the *Mass Line* system, a Western character like James Bond could turn into a world leader and a role model. The dictator's propaganda machinery took the karaoke form, whereas entertainment for the people was a cheap Western copy of a Beijing opera.

Mass Line was distinctly political and yet at the same time it was a highly poetic performance mostly based on my own observations and experience of living in a closed country. We played with large political and social systems that we all had to follow in order to be part of the group. These are systems, whose intentions are to keep us occupied, to act properly and keep us in line. In countries with powerful leadership and control system people used to pretend, to be someone different in public than at home. Everyone became an actor ready to stage what the system expected from them, performing ideologies as one's second nature. And this was a wise survival tactic for everyday life. In the end it is impossible to decide what is a performance and what is authentic.

In my work *A Room of One's Own*, a video and photo installation from 2011, I tried to find out how much space was left for a woman as a mother and a wife in a new suburban family house. It seems that women and femininity are determined by space—think of the communal flats in the Soviet Union or the one-family suburban homes in America in the 1950s (the Estonian equivalent is the early twenty-first century houses built in the fields close to the city). The Soviet woman did not need much space at home, because she was mostly away at work. The American woman as a mother and a wife did not need separate space as she was there to serve others. Virginia Woolf stated once that a woman must have money and a room of her own if she is to write fiction.

Women are shown their place by way of space, or as Julia Kristeva said, femininity can be understood as a position in the border areas. At the same time the new influences enter any culture, namely through the borders. Working with the woman-space relations I have begun to see more clearly how unconscious and silent power lines determine the behavioral patterns of men and women and their spatial positions. Estonian women want to live in the American dream, but to achieve it, they have to work in town, send their children to kindergartens in town, as there are no such establishments near where they live, the nearest shop and even the bus stop are miles away.

As a spatial installation, *A Room of One's Own* was furnished as a typically cramped sitting room in a new residential area, where the viewer sees the photographs of the mother, and the TV-monitors alternating with women dancing in a winter landscape. One's own room in the title does not tell us whose room it is, if it belongs to a man or a woman. In the text, Woolf tells about a place where a woman can be on her own, which disrupts her daily chores and makes room for reflection. Like an artist's studio, a room of her own is essential for a woman who wants to write. This room means a disruption of the mundane, and although it is furnished modestly as a sitting-room, it is a place that reflects the joy of life, because, according to Woolf, a writer struggling in the shackles of hatred and worry cannot create anything eternal.

The main link of the inhabitants of the new residential settlements to the outside world, except their office and kindergarten in town, is television, the larger the better. It is so big that their neighbors across the road have no need to switch theirs on. These women are happy; most of them have a job and a peaceful, safe home, even if storms cause occasional power cuts. These women have their own houses, which means they have a lot more space. However, this space is furnished in a very similar way. The houses bought with the young family loans, feature an open kitchen, so that mothers could see what the children are doing. These women are constantly available to their families, they lack any private space. I found that the real masters of the house are the children. Incidentally, quite a few of these women, with a varying shade of red hair, were reading the book *Eat. Pray. Love* by Elizabeth Gilbert (amazing, we were born on the same day!).

Artist Sirje Ainso from the Estonian diaspora in Argentina who saw the installation in the Estonian pavilion at the Venice Art Biennale in 2011 decided that I had Soviet nostalgia and I was showing Estonia in a regretful manner: "How does the described represent Estonia . . . ? Does the artist's topic with a 'social message' justify this display, which shows Estonia in a worse light than any 'fourth world' country, where nobody wants to go? . . . Unfortunately, the artist has

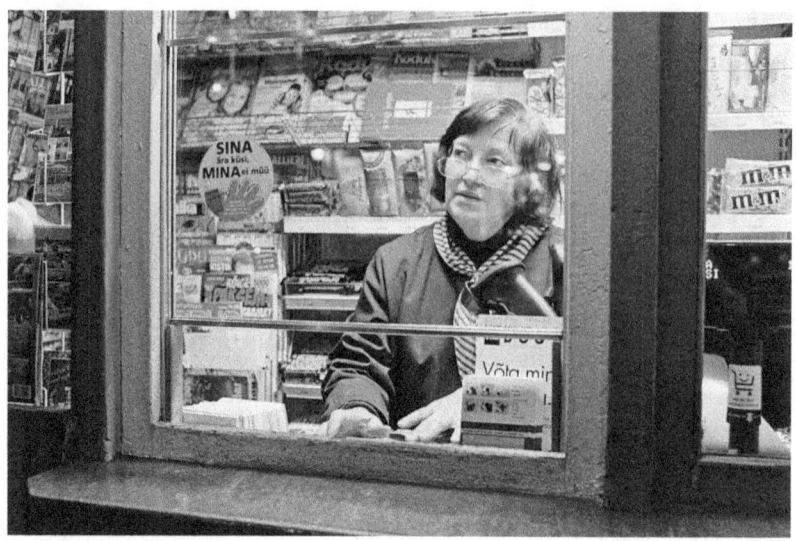

FIG. 3.2 Liina Siib, *A Woman Takes Little Space*. Ongoing series since 2007. Digitally edited analogue color photography, pigmented ink print, 30 cm × 45 cm. Courtesy of the artist.

despite her education and today's opportunities, both feet still firmly planted in the Soviet era—is this inertia or nostalgia . . . ? Too bad this chance to present Estonia as a cultured country was lost."

In 2007 I began the photographic series *A Woman Takes Little Space* as a reaction to the debate in the media about the gender-based discrimination and pay gap. According to EU statistics, in Estonia the unadjusted gender pay gap was 30.9 percent in 2007, which was the highest in the EU and until now, it still is. The less paid labor sectors in Estonia are also mostly occupied by female employees: textile industry, cleaning service, social welfare, sport, amusement and leisure activities, food and drink services, social and cultural institutions (archives, libraries, museums, etc.), retail trade and catering establishments.

I met nearly all of the women "who take little space" by chance in public spaces. Mostly they were strangers, and in some cases they remained so, although I always made a point of asking their permission and explain why I needed that picture: to show a working woman via space. I take these photographs in order to make certain situations visible. Estonian women occasionally seem to be too well adapted to the model of working women, which is prescribed by gender roles.

Their professional identity is largely shaped by their employer, who arranges the workplace for women employees depending on the nature of their work and never thinking of women themselves. Due to submissiveness and low self-esteem, the women never complain about their working conditions. The retirees, the temporary employed, or those fearing to be made redundant are not going to take any risks. Many jobs with dismal conditions and low salary are taken up by Russian-speaking women. When I was taking the pictures, I naturally asked myself, "What can a woman do in a situation like this?"

Thus, I started wondering what the situation is like for building coalitions, solidarity, benevolent and trust-respect relationships at the working place in the circumstances of precarious labor and in the society that mostly praises success and individuality. Considering differences as a resource of power, performing mutual empowerment can raise the courage to stand firm for one's rights, including the rights for gender equality. Solidarity presumes an ability to communicate and, following Karl Marx, space plays an important role in the development of the social consciousness, as through communication the groups can prove their solidarity to others. The contemporary precarious work creates migrant spaces. Whatever the space, one needs to expand it for relations, bonds, links that can bring any groups of inequality together—for support, humor, sympathy, and solidarity against the market and the philosophy of profit which erase our humanity every second and in every aspect. To find a balance between "*solidaire*" and "*solitaire*."

TLOSTANOVA: What strikes me in most of your work is a subtle and multilayered irony, a cunning tongue-in-cheek rendering of often painful and cruel subjects, which in my perception is similar to the Armenian Queering Yerevan Collective's tactic of slant activism. (Instead of confronting the patriarchal and heteronormative state head-on, the members of this collective use indirect, ironic, double-entendre ways of making their political and aesthetic statements.) In your fascinating project *A Woman Takes Little Space* you apply irony very effectively, weaving it through your complex reflections on the prescribed women's roles, unchanging under any regimes (democratic or autocratic), the curse of muteness and submissiveness and various ways of going around and beyond it, the inescapable objectification, and creativity and freedom crammed into constrained spatial conditions in both literal and figurative sense. Do you think then that irony is more effective than any blunt collision with, or resistance to power and authority? Do you see irony as a powerful decolonizing force?

SIIB: Oh, I did not know about the Queering Yerevan Collective's work before. *A Woman Takes Little Space* depicts quite different women in their working environment. Sometimes they argued that there was nothing particular in them, that there was no point in taking pictures of them. They did not consider the image of a working woman to be worthwhile or beautiful. And so there are not many images of women in their workplaces in today's media, except when a business goes bust. At the same time I do not want to repeat the ideological construction where human beings in their daily situation are placed in a heroic presented as victims. As for situations, it was important that a point in the passing randomness momentarily touched upon a point in myself, has made me identify with a person and a situation. It is a subjective sympathy of a sort. A woman becomes an actor who plays her own life, as in a neo-realist approach. Most of the represented women have had a good sense of humor that was reflected in the photographs as well. Humor attracts humor? Isn't it a possibility for a coalition?!

But, yes, irony has also been with me as long as I remember. For me it has been difficult to be solemn, serious, even in the hardest situations, even when dealing with the subject that I do care and am serious about. But the tactics, the approach . . . . Yes, it is something else. Recently I have been thinking critically about my ironic position. Why am I ironical, even cynical, in some works? Maybe it has to do with the language; maybe the bitter truth is easier to convey through humor or satire. Maybe this is an inseparable part of me as a "post-socialist" subject. People who have lived under totalitarian regimes acquire a bred-in-the-bone irony as part of their survival strategy.

I elaborated on this theme in my video work *Compromise Excluded*, in which illusion and reality were hopelessly and schizophrenically mixed, but the possible fictitiousness of situations was quite deceptive. It grew out of pervasive violence that occurred in recent Estonian history. The heroes were extremists, the totalitarian left- and right-wingers, Communists and Fascists who rejected pluralism and

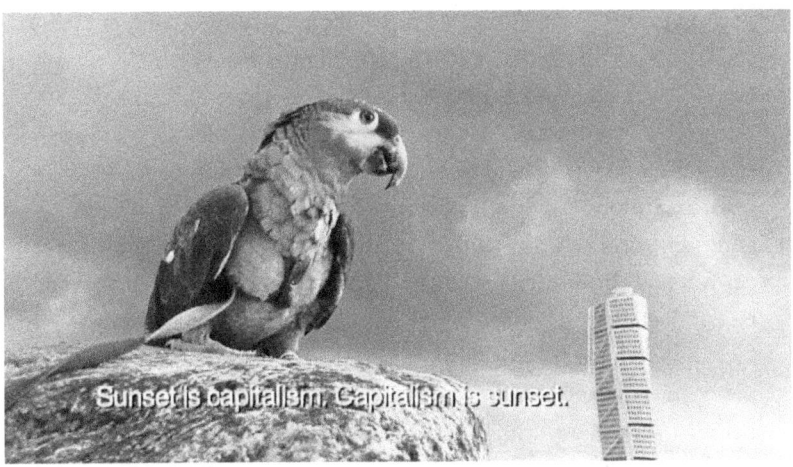

Sunset is capitalism. Capitalism is sunset.

FIG. 3.3 Liina Siib, still image at 12 minutes, 41 seconds from the video *Mass Line: Office 1*. 2013. Produced by Lilith Performance Studio, Malmö, Sweden. Courtesy of the artist.

detested democratic processes. The videos mostly explored the well-known places of aggression and executions. Here the location itself became one of the characters in the story. Irony comes into play when reality cannot be reasonably signified; when truth and lies are hopelessly confused. Irony, then, is a signifying practice, an action. The absurd is even more an action than irony. I really like the Dadaist practices and have come to do similar things myself more often. It also seems that putting together the high and the low is often rewarding.

There is a problem with irony: it somehow offers a safe position, a safe distance between the subject and the audience. It confirms the existing patterns. This has made me think if I am really doing justice to my subjects this way. I have used the irony consciously as a figure of speech, as my rhetoric that enables me to perform a montage-like representation, with juxtapositions and counterpoints. Who knows, maybe humor is a better way to stress the empathy. An ironic person remains a passive bystander; all she can do is to bitterly sneer at the hopeless circumstances and situations. A different thing would be to take irony to a totally new level, because in the new brave world of bureaucrats, we are facing the new totalitarianism, and here something has to be done without mercy.

TLOSTANOVA: For me, you are a paradigmatic border person in the sense that you do not seem to belong in either of the many worlds along which you travel. Yet you travel along these different worlds, not necessarily human (but maybe companion species), and sometimes quite marginal and forbidden for many other people, with an open and interested mind and with a loving perception, as María Lugones once said. At the same time, there is a certain detachment, a certain additional dimension always present in your optics. It could be connected with your many travels abroad as well as with the very fact that you are an artist who never entirely belongs and is always between different worlds, and therefore sees more than those who belong to just one world. At times it seems that you look even at yourself from aside. Still, I would like to ask you if there are any important anchors for your soul, to paraphrase Salman Rushdie, such as language, place, customs or people, that would help you define your belonging, or you feel yourself entirely a worldly person even if physically you may continue living in Estonia? In general, is such a belonging and feeling at home important for you? Or these are outdated concepts?

SIIB: Anchors—outdated or not—I do feel cosmopolitan for sure. My family has kept me in Estonia, the graves of my ancestors. I am as morbid as any proper Estonian who has plenty of funeral photos in their family albums: grandmothers, grandfathers, the father, the mother. My mother died this summer (2015) and after her death the feeling of being a complete "stranger" here has strongly struck me. It seems like with my mother, I have lost my country, although a citizen, I have become a mental refugee. But fortunately I still have very good friends that make me feel at home. Friendships really matter. And sometimes I remember that it was certainly the highlight of my life when the iron curtain fell, we could finally travel and Estonia regained its independence. Freedom is the main thing. The possibility to decide on my own and to make my own choices. And always reminding myself of resistance.

I have always liked the fable by Jean de La Fontaine "The Wolf and The Dog," where the latter praises his good life and almost convinces the Wolf. But suddenly the Wolf detects a galled spot on his neck:

"What's that?" he cries. "Oh, nothing but a speck . . .

Perhaps the collar's mark by which they chain me."

"Chain! Chain you! What! Run you not, then,
Just where you please and when?"
"Not always, sir; but what of that?"
"Enough for me, to spoil your fat!" . . . !" . . .

I like languages—if I did not become an artist, I would have wished to become a linguist. I do feel belonging to nature and to culture, certainty to the art community. Films, books, everyday practices and history are all part of my homeland, as well as teaching at the art academy, discussing contemporary art context. And there is some idiosyncrasy in my works that reappears again and again, like the social aspects of life in a society and its margins—the people.

Looking at myself from aside—I remember doing this already from my childhood—I have always looked at myself with someone else's eyes. This knowledge has not made me happier though. I try to keep things dynamic, to see what happens, acting by nonacting. It is difficult to take seriously anything that becomes a system or a method that becomes orthodox, and quite often a belonging to any group can become just that—a frozen orthodoxy. I do not go to the barricades, but rather to the outskirts, to observe how the other half lives. There are too many themes, but they keep repeating like the places on my photos—graveyards, ships, and prisons. . . .

TLOSTANOVA: How would you define the political potential of art in today's world? Is art less or more effective than social movements or critical theories in changing reality and the way people think and see the world? What is a political art for you? Should art be political at all and in what ways if so? Godard once said that instead of making political films he wants to make films politically. Do you think it is an important distinction today? Or maybe ethical and other dimensions are more important for art than politics?

SIIB: The political potential of art and the possibility of choosing the tools for the politics of representation is something that seems always to be present in art as one of its important characteristics. When there is "us" and "them," there is always politics, a political situation. In repressive ideological environments, even escapist art can declare a certain politics. In today's world the amount of information is immense and it is easy to lose one's sight and mind, not to mention one's focus. It is easier to turn to entertainment, but even in that sphere there are political avenues. How then can we shape a lucid artistic position, how can we keep it in accordance with the dynamics of time and how not to become an opportunist willing to grab the "urgent" and "burning" issues for easy political profit? These are the questions and the hard work to accomplish.

There are at least two kinds of political connotations in any artwork: first, the immediate reaction to everyday reality, and second, the hidden layers that only begin to speak when time passes by. I doubt that much of the Soviet time resistance art would have the same significance for today's viewer as it used to be in the closed society with its doublespeak. Yet if an avant-garde resisting art piece will be hung alongside the mainstream commissioned politically correct art work, the intelligent viewer would hopefully detect the difference, the boundary between the truth and the lie, and also see the different regimes of representation. Of course, here irony is a catalyst. Good art always has several layers and if done honestly with one's heart and mind, the new layers of meaning will emerge and manifest the latent political agenda in a new context.

Art as any other form within a culture should aim for critical attitude and signification, for the new forms, for a contemporary moment, for resistance to stagnation. Art should aim to exist alongside with reality in order to influence it and—who knows?—maybe also change this reality, because changes always start from the tiniest things. The best thing to do is to be responsible, honest to oneself and to speak with and to the society. Even if the society does not care immediately, one still has to continue speaking.

With the hegemony of images and cultural consumption, art certainly has more impact as a (cultural) product, yet well-made and curated exhibitions create spaces for thinking and sharing and inspire new ideas. Art is the last island for transgression in the politically correct world. It is trying out and expanding the borders of human existence and freedom. There could be mutual empowerment among artists and people they work with that I find important and essential.

Godard saying he wants to make films politically could mean the same thing about representation—either the work of art is a representation of politics (as there are so many commissioned works and works made under various totalitarian regimes, the ideological art) or it shows the politics of representation, when the personal becomes the political. Every artist has to find a balance here, to answer these questions for themselves. And sometimes the work made innocently can become a political statement as well, no matter how humble was the initial idea of an artist. Ethical implications are certainly important and making art should not harm (physically or psychologically) anyone involved in the project. In this respect any artist has to show responsibility. On the other hand, as I mentioned before, art is the last space of transgression which is left today, the space where the craziest ideas can be explored and implemented. Anyway, artists should try to avoid the social blindness as much as possible, and should address urgent problems with their oeuvres. To be present and to swim against the current.

TLOSTANOVA: In our conversation in Tallinn, you mentioned that you are now fascinated with factories. Can you elaborate a little bit on why factories attract your attention as an artist in this notorious postindustrial age?

SIIB: As an art student in the late 1980s, we had a compulsory internship at different factories to draw and paint the working process and the factory environments. Although the views were rather grim, badly lit, with oppressive conditions, I was still quite fascinated with the conveyor system and the grandeur of space, the production scale and sounds. In 1998 I made a series *Le Carceri* in an abandoned cellulose factory in Tallinn where space played the most important role as an imaginary architecture of a sacred and notorious post-industrialist place.

In a way, technology and production are quite in place in the agenda of graphic arts and printmaking. Some ten years ago I taught a course called "Human being and factory" for the graphic department of the art academy; the title refers ironically to the Soviet period theme art exhibitions which were held annually. Back then artists had to show their connection with the working people, no matter was it really their commitment or not. It was done for the representation of politics. So I decided to examine what has happened to the factories in the post-industrial time and how the proletariat looked in the 2000s.

Together with the students we visited several bigger factories in Tallinn. It was an interesting mapping, to see how the analogue technologies have given way to the highly computerized processes with fewer workers, and how the old work benches existed side by side with computers. Walter Benjamin wrote on the special aura in "The Work of Art in the Age of Mechanical Reproduction." I think that one can also speak of the aura of production sites. But their reproduction is another thing—at least in photography, and here something has to be constructed, as Benjamin states in his essay talking about the Krupp factories. The aspect of this "something" which "has to be constructed" was initially proposed by Bertolt Brecht, because the reproduction of reality hardly says anything about reality which is an important factor to consider also in terms of political art. Later I reshaped the course for the "twenty-first century worker" and made a visual research survey through time from the beginning of the twentieth century with its Fordist and Soviet industrial ideas until nowadays.

TLOSTANOVA: Looking back at your different works, you have been dealing with a diverse array of subjects from gender to alienation and loneliness, from gazing to precariousness, from growing social gaps and exclusion to the contradictions and the darker sides of childhood, from the economy of public and private spaces to the mechanics of memory and especially embodied memory, and much more. What are you interested in and what have you found important to address today?

SIIB: Too many things. Nowadays, I am continuing with the same interests and themes—in an altered way, perhaps, but the subjects I address are still the same: injustice, social haunting, struggles for survival, ideological constructions, conformity, and compromises. What does it mean to be human? Perhaps I have adopted a more active position, bringing into the exhibition performative approaches, interactions, the process itself rather than the end product of art. I implement my observations and visual and photographic notes in performances and reenactments, thus rebuilding the situations.

Aristotle said that in order to remember things we need a place. Places as empty stages incite the viewer's imagination. Forgetting is not enough to overcome a difficult burden, because everything comes back sooner or later. Memory lets itself be repressed to a certain extent. But then it turns into a creative starting point. The process of reenacting historical events in contemporary settings, imbuing them with new meanings, offers a new chance for something already forgotten, loading it with a contemporary moment. This is important as it can help make the work comprehensible to the audience. There must be contemporary elements in the works in order to make them relevant or even urgent in today's situations.

Theoretically, I have been lately interested in emblems and how images repeat themselves through history, how society is constructed and how it consciously and unconsciously influences our minds and ideologies, how people perform their everyday lives, the remains of rituals, emptied of any significance or any principal idea. Practically, visualizing resistance is something with which I would like to go on, to study and comment on it. Two sentences describing our contemporary condition keep haunting me:

1) "Everyone wants to survive."
2) "One has to hide emotions in order to keep the job."

Even I myself was told some months ago by a colleague at the art academy that I am too emotional. So I think I have to do something with emotions, too. And affects.

What is urgent is how to remain an ethical human being, how to save human space, empathy, solidarity, benevolence. In the global world where everyone is trying to survive, it is easy to become blind toward certain groups, classes, phenomena that are just outside the focus. It is easy to start living in one's bubble. What remains significant over time? One's body, freedom of choice and speech, the joy of living (*joie de vivre*), and one's home.

CHAPTER FOUR

Beyond Dependencies: A Talk with Vyacheslav Akhunov,
the Lonely Ranger of Uzbek Contemporary Art

MADINA TLOSTANOVA: In a number of present day authoritarian
states, succeeding the USSR, once again, the power dictates the artists what their art should be like. What changes is only the ideological stuffing (usually, there is a shift to a hysterical national patriotic
mood), while the mechanisms of imposing unanimous thinking and
unanimous stylistics remain largely the same. In the USSR the artists
reacted to this pressure among other things, through the underground
movement, and you have acted as one of the important underground
artists. Do you think that a second edition of the underground is possible today on the remnants of the Soviet empire, including a revival of
its importance and influence? Or it is not possible to step twice into
the same river, and the time, the context and the people have changed
so much that the presence of the underground ambience (such as the
apartment exhibitions) does not automatically mean that the spirit
of the underground is back?

VYACHESLAV AKHUNOV: The difference between the underground
in the USSR and the art of postcolonial Uzbekistan is enormous, in

spite of the fact that the Soviet totalitarian system has not been dismantled in Uzbekistan. In the USSR the available information was so carefully filtered that any sources or true facts related to the modernist art, were practically inaccessible. Paradoxically, this serious shortage of knowledge generated persistent efforts to find information that would not be infected by ideological clichés. Some of it could be fished out from books and articles written by the Soviet art critics who specialized in the criticism of bourgeois art from the viewpoint of the Marxist-Leninist aesthetics.

An artist who was the first to find information on this or that modernist movement, could then quickly apply it to his own work, adding some local Soviet features as well, and even be considered a rather advanced Soviet modernist. This is what happened in the "nonconformist" context, for example in the works of Oscar Rabin, who was under the influence of René Magritte, or Ilya Kabakov who was strongly influenced by Joseph Kosuth. In other words we are speaking here of rediscovering Western modernist art in the hermetic totalitarian society, isolated from the rest of the world by the "iron curtain." In reality, for the USSR this was a time of discovery of the white spots on the map of the world art. And this process generated a great thirst and willingness to see the forbidden and inaccessible with one's own eyes, even if it was only mediated by our own Soviet artists. Following jazz, blues, rock-n-roll, Pepsi Cola and jeans the USSR was penetrated by the contemporary Western art. Interestingly enough, this art had not reached the Soviet capitals of Central Asia and Kazakhstan to such an extent that it could trigger a self-organization of even a small group of nonconformist artists, or could lead to an emergence of the underground and its typical exhibition practices in the form of apartment and closed exhibitions, Samizdat and various dissident activities.

From 1973 to 1980, as a student of the Moscow Art Institute I had to go back and forth two or three times a year from Central Asia to Moscow. When I started making conceptual art I wanted to find like-minded people in my native Kirgizia and in Uzbekistan. But I could not find them either in Tashkent, or in Fergana and Frunze. There were no underground writers, poets, artists or film directors. Later I understood that in the logic of Empire, every thinking individual was striving to get out of the provincial oppression and get settled in the metropolis ("All the best for the capital of the empire!" The food, the advanced technologies, the best specialists, theaters, actors, museums, libraries and so on). It was not a secret that many parents were dreaming of sending their children to study in the metropolis so that later they could somehow manage to stay there for good. Today the rich Western countries are an attractive place for people with extraordinary abilities, but in those times such a place was the Empire's capital. Having become the "Muscovites," the former provincial people were able to raise their status, particularly in the eyes of those compatriots who were left on the outskirts of the evil empire. The presence of the diplomatic corps and foreign embassies, of the Soviet specialists who worked abroad and foreign students—all that was the source of information which created an appropriate climate for the "small breakthroughs," particularly in culture and art. In contrast with the metropolis the provinces lacked many privileges and first of all, information.

The Moscow underground was comprised of both the local artists and the ones who came from the provincial places. Inquisitive minds from the Asian republics, Kazakhstan, the Caucasus, from such regions as Siberia, the Urals, the Far East, and the South of Russia were excluded from the nonconformist art process unless they moved to Moscow. They did it for many reasons and primarily in the quest of an environment consisting of the like-minded people, a context in which their works would be recognized and cause reflection.

In 1979 I wrote the following words: "A new époque has come— the époque of developed socialism, which allows for the discussion of various problems and problematization in art. Today the Soviet art is divided into the official and nonofficial, or in the opinion of those in power, into the correct and incorrect art. The correct is the socialist realism and the incorrect is all the rest, which does not focus on ideology but on Western modernism instead. There emerged such concepts as "us" and "them" (same and other, native and foreign). We are the correct ones. They are incorrect, the bad guys, almost traitors of the homeland, enemies and renegades. And no cultural dialogue is possible between us and them, between the Soviet us and the Western others. They are with others, and we are against them— this is the logic of the representatives of the official art. The internal multicultural context in the Soviet art was constructed according to the formula "national in its form and socialist in its essence."

In the present day Uzbekistan the situation is different:

1) There is no hunger for information anymore. Any information on contemporary art is available now including political activism in art forms.
2) It is possible to freely choose as your artistic priority any "-ism," to create and exhibit your works.
3) The artist is allowed to travel anywhere.

Yet each of these new freedoms has its "but" . . . It is all allowed and possible only up to the point when an artist's work approaches a boundary behind which there starts a discussion of the social and political problems of contemporary Uzbekistan.

If the Moscow artistic underground of the 1960–1970s was predominantly interested in innovative modernist forms which in the conditions of the Cold War was in itself considered a serious political mishap, today it is the artists and the political activists who comprise the underground. There are reasons for that. Art is in a different situation. Due to the impossibility of producing new forms, the main concern is representation and not innovation. The medium has to switch all the efforts towards the representation of the message using the old signs put together in different new combinations. Then the artistic innovation as a revelation of Truth is not possible. Focusing on representation, particularly of political discourse, transfers the responsibility for innovation to the audience, making it a co-participant in the art process equally responsible for its results. In other words, we have a situation in which art (in this case, politically active art) is not created for the people, but rather is completely delegated to the people who decide themselves what to choose.

The main representations are the art forms connected with actionism, happening, performance, which require a space and an audience. This does not always fit into the idea of apartment exhibitions. Today an apartment exhibition can exist in a different format when an artist makes a performance at some place, and hundreds of spectators can stay home and watch the action on-line or share with each other their own mini apartment exhibitions which due to censorship could not get to any official museum space.

But we are speaking of a rather small group of politically active artists. While the majority remains ignorant. Consider the fact that all the graduates of the Uzbek Art Institute who were sent to continue their studies in Europe (similarly to the Soviet Union where people were sent to study in Moscow and Leningrad on the national quota) came back not knowing what is modernism and contemporary art. A 150-year period of art history has remained unknown to them. They never learned to speak the language of modernity and express what is of current interest. "We were studying the great legacy of the Renaissance masters,"—was their answer. They are disgusted and annoyed with contemporary art as an expression of liberal European values, because instead of studying the contemporaneity they were busy reading the hackneyed recipes from the old art cook book. Here, among the provincial artistic plankton, they feel at ease. This is not a colonial legacy, rather it is an effect of reflection—an internal colonization of the country and the people as a result of the continuous Soviet phobias of the Uzbek political leadership.

In a totalitarian state where society is held together by fear and national-patriotic propaganda, there is no space for contemporary art. The official artistic community and the "Academy of Arts" work for maintaining the myth that both national and contemporary art doesn't only exist, but also flourish pretending that such artistic forums as the Tashkent biennial of contemporary art, plays an important role in the life of society and the state. Largely it is a self-deception strategy.

TLOSTANOVA: In several interviews you speak of your rejection or at least, a very cautious attitude to tradition as it is understood in the official aesthetics imposed from above. You link tradition—interpreted in such a way—with an inescapable second-handedness of cultural production in the post-Soviet countries. It seems to me that this can be called a colonized consciousness and perception, and today more often, it is a voluntary self-colonization. Yet, do you believe there is some other, not necessarily tradition (as in my view this word itself is too negatively overloaded from the start and marked as stagnant, dark and bad in comparison with modernity), but maybe some system of aesthetic notions which would be different from the global unified production and also from the local provincial and distorted understanding of national culture and mentality, seen as detached from the course of time and from the needs and wishes of the real people? And if such an open and flexible system does exist after all,

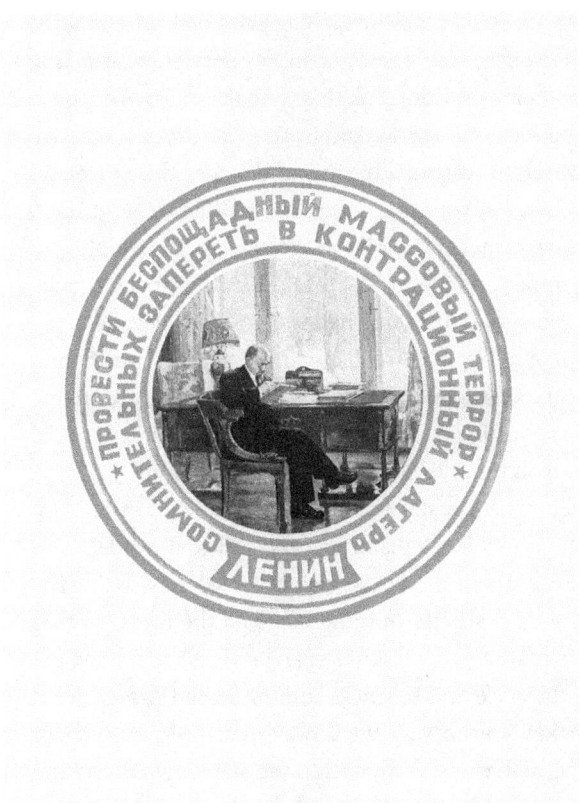

FIG. 4.1
Vyacheslav Akhu-
nov, *USSR Stamps
and Seals* (Lenin:
To conduct a mer-
ciless mass terror.
To lock the suspi-
cious in the con-
centration camps.)
1977. Paper, serial
print, watercolor,
40 cm × 29.5 cm.
Courtesy of the
artist.

at least potentially, should the artists turn to it and remake it? And if yes then how, in what forms?

AKHUNOV: Let us first remember the history: In the nineteen twenties there were efforts to create a revolutionary Central Asian art of avant-garde type by means of subleasing the "second futurist coming" (Alexander Volkov and others).[1] By the early 1930s an artistic system with Socialist realist definitions (such as futurological utopia) was forcefully imposed. Its local departments were created within one state organization—the Artists' Union with the headquarters in the capital of the Empire. From this center all the appropriate recommendations, orders, and instructions were dispatched to all regional and ethnic-national cultural centers of the country, up to the indications of what topics to explore and in what realistic manner to depict them.

All of these processes had a clear ideologically determined goal: to help the party to remake (colonize) people's consciousness taking into account their local conditions, that is to make a new identity, a Soviet person, a builder of communism in the context of the active destruction of age-old traditions. In several decades the Soviet art had developed a Socialist tradition with its own hierarchy. In fact, what the Czarist government did not manage to do in its colonies (to colonize people's minds and feelings) in almost sixty years of its rule, the communist ideologues accomplished in just three decades. The ideological discourse of Socialist realism corrupted the culture and art of all the countries that belonged to the Socialist camp, drawing them into the funnel of hypocrisy and carrion and causing a social and spiritual duality in the artists' minds and imaginations.

Have the Uzbek artists really reconsidered after becoming "independent" the "age old local historical and cultural models and the almost hundred years of the Soviet tradition?" Hardly so . . . The artists with the Soviet aesthetic training changed the faces, clothes and names of their characters, but otherwise the vector remained the same: they make the state and business commissioned works, focus on sales, local market, and serving the power structures. Indeed, for those who are used to live and work within the state regulations and under the spell of the outdated notions, it is hardly possible to risk a step towards any creative independence.

In the 1990s, when the Soviet restrictions were lifted, the majority of artists never managed to find a new place in the unknown and hence uncomfortable cultural environment. Having lost the dismantled Artists' Union, they did not strive for the emergence of any independent creative groups and unions based on their shared specific professional ethics and contemporary aesthetic contexts. On the contrary, they wanted to be united once again into yet another agency organized by the top-down directive.

And what about the new generations of artists who have not experienced the horrors of the totalitarian regime but gladly play the game imposed by the state? What makes them so sluggish in their quest for a new language? Hardly can we interpret this as an expression of some internal instinct, which developed due to local historical, religious, philosophic or aesthetic traditions. But the Soviet tradition as we know not only destroyed all local models, but also carefully protected the common people and the artists from the alien social constructs and from some feeble efforts to build a new aesthetic reality.

Nevertheless, one can trace a delayed line in the works of Uzbek artists—originally a protest line which was completely exhausted by the 1970s–80s. It was shaped as an interest in the Oriental practices such as Sufism, Daoism, and Zen-Buddhism. We should remember that the Sufi concept of the "ideal human being" and its doctrine of moral perfection were at one point regarded as Muslim ideological opposition, and today plays the part of the spiritual and ethical opposition to the existing authoritarian regime. Yet what in the USSR was an alternative to the Soviet ideology and therefore was banned, today is no longer a threat to the dominant discourse, which is working for the creation of the national patriotic narrative. The administration even restores the monuments on Sufi graves and many Sufis are now considered the national spiritual heroes.

The postmodernist époque considerably smoothed out the boundaries between the so-called Eastern-oriented and Western-oriented artists. The artists' demands reach far beyond their local, regional boundaries. They are no longer interested in external, often exotic sides of their culture. There is a deeply grounded wish to get to the roots. In such a context, a propensity for one's own tradition, not enriched by the worldly experience, becomes a dead-end in the artist's quest and development. It is useless to break lances on what is today an Uzbek artist—an "Asian type," a "European type," or some variety of Eurasianism.

There is a threatening pressure of the never dismantled past on the present. But how deeply does the splinter of passeism sit in the unconsciousness of Uzbek artists? I think that there has never been such a penchant for the past, such conservatism, such a hostile attitude to contemporary art—for those who even in the Soviet times managed to find the boldest and most extraordinary creative decisions. Their spiritual and plastic quests have always taken unusual routes and they are the least prone to the influences of the olden times or someone else's ideas and notions.

The technology of colonization of people's minds has remained the same as a legacy of the previous colonial system, but today we are speaking of the internal self-colonization as a result of the lacking decolonization processes. Up to now the majority of the citizens considers Uzbekistan a remaining part of the former Soviet Union, a "USSR reserve." Partly such a reflection is linked to the fact that most of the people who live in Uzbekistan lack any national identity.

The mixture of the Soviet and the post-Soviet combined with the lack of any creative and intelligent specialists from any area (from cultural studies to sociology, history, art, literature and up to the ideologues and political scientists) at the service of power, falsifications of history through a forceful erasing of the collective memory—all this has generated a provincial and distorted understanding of national culture, and as a result—a cultural decline. In the end the people and the country are offered a simulacrum of culture and art, a semblance of poorly masked primitive wild capitalism, a group in power who is far from people's interests, a noncompetitive economy, and the hastily masked social problems which can easily turn into political.

In these conditions no breakthrough to a higher social, political or cultural level is possible. Neither is it possible to work for the creation of a system of aesthetic notions answering the present conditions and national features. We need intellectuals whose deficit have already become customary, and we need a will of the ruling elite. Every person's contribution is important if this person is able to create a globally competitive product, thus attracting the attention to the history, culture and the problems of our country [Uzbekistan]. The more such people emerge (scholars, cultural activists, artists, specialists of the highest rank in different spheres of human activity), the more chances there would be to take the country out of its stagnation. Such individuals have discovered an open and flexible system of aesthetic notions which can function in the conditions of escaping the discipline of power structures in the detached and free border space. As a result something new can emerge in the end.

TLOSTANOVA: In a number of your texts you mention the original and independent style of "Socialist modernism" that started to be shaped in the end of the Soviet period, yet, due to the well-known historical events, was later wrapped up and sadly replaced with neocolonial mimicking styles and repetitions of someone else's ideas. Can a new and original style emerge today similar to Socialist modernism and if yes, what would be its main strategies, techniques and nodal points? Or all the points of nonreturn are already passed and contemporary art from the ex-Soviet countries is indeed doomed? Your own work has successfully testified the opposite demonstrating that Uzbekistan does have contemporary art. Which artists do you find the most representative of the post-Soviet human condition?

AKHUNOV: For the original style or a new artistic trend to emerge, a border situation is necessary when the old cannot exist anymore and the wind of change is breaking into the entrance door. Of course the old should be able to help develop the new. As I said earlier, today the main concern is representation and not innovation due to a complete exhaustion of the form-building process. In the absence of such process, it is impossible for the new phenomena to emerge. Hence, no fundamentally new subjective idea which needs a new subjective form for its realization is possible. The old art system is completely exhausted and there are no premises yet for the emergence of the new one. We must remember that artists have nothing left but to find courage in themselves to claim their rights to a subjective view of the world, to an "object," to a hope that their "object" will come back. Unfortunately, contemporary art of the ex-Soviet countries is doomed to stay at the end of the list because today contemporary Western artists are backed up by the new and powerful technologies, a developed infrastructure of culture and art, and substantial financial investments.

The nodal points would remain the same—the anthropological points, the human being and human agency. The strategies would vary. The heroes would be both individual and collective. It is hard for me to define who the most important artists are for the understanding of the post-Soviet human condition. I rather prefer the intellectual curators who are able to identify the social and political sores and choose from a mass of projects, the most topical artistic works that discuss the urgent problems of society, in order to bring them tactfully together into a large multimedia orchestra and represent this multimedia symphony to the audiences. Viktor Misiano is one of them.

As for the neocolonial mimicking styles and repetition of someone else's ideas, the contemporary art movement in Central Asia, which receives enough Western grants, definitely looks derivative and second-rate if not third-rate in comparison with Western art. It is its pseudo-copy. But no one seems to be preoccupied with this. The new heroes of contemporary art first attempted to exploit the ethnographic effect—their national features sprinkled with stereo-typical depictions of the post-Soviet social life. This dish was served to the Western audience as a substitute for real action. But a new time has come and demanded to discard this ersatz and copying, for the sake of real art, thus proving the poor judgment of Central Asian contemporary artists who hastily mended their worn-out orien-tal clothes to make them look more like Western fashions. Ridicu-lous rags à la dervish, supposedly liberated cynical nomadism, low taste buffoonery—allowed the capricious and slippery West to look at Central Asian contemporary artists with sarcasm as if they were some curious mimicking creatures speaking an incoherent language, and thoughtlessly imitating someone else's gestures.

The arbitrary appropriation of aesthetic practices and elements of language—not only intensified the problem of identity (without an identity rooted in the native culture one cannot hope to find any inter-est or understanding in the world) but also exposed the neocolonialist politics—the ubiquitous Western cultural expansion. It is not really clear what is better—the Uzbek pragmatic apathy or the post-Soviet Asian third-rate pseudo-copies and an urge to prove one's otherness by any means, for instance, by appropriating someone else's experience in the hope of being accepted. The artist has been taken to the level of expandable material and the third-rate imitating époque has stimu-lated a new artistic system. It continues to represent itself as socially concerned art, but in reality an active export of postmodernist copies has long become an indicative feature of cultural neocolonialism.

Now let me say a few words on the Socialist modernism. In the 1970s a number of critically minded artists decided to destroy the habitual order and combine the communist ideological artistic paradigm with the modernist creation of new forms that is to synthesize the Socialist realism and the modernist discourse. It was a bold attempt to create an artistic trend of Socialist modernism as a combination of the aestheti-cally politicized Soviet and Western art and thus pull the canonized and exhausted Socialist realism out of its stagnation. It was necessary to create a new avant-garde reality in new artistic gestures, languages and forms. The question arose: what methods, forms and meanings were to be used to de-ideologize the Soviet art? Gradually out of smaller movements the general concept of Socialist modernism started to emerge. The name itself was uneasy: "Socialist" did not go together

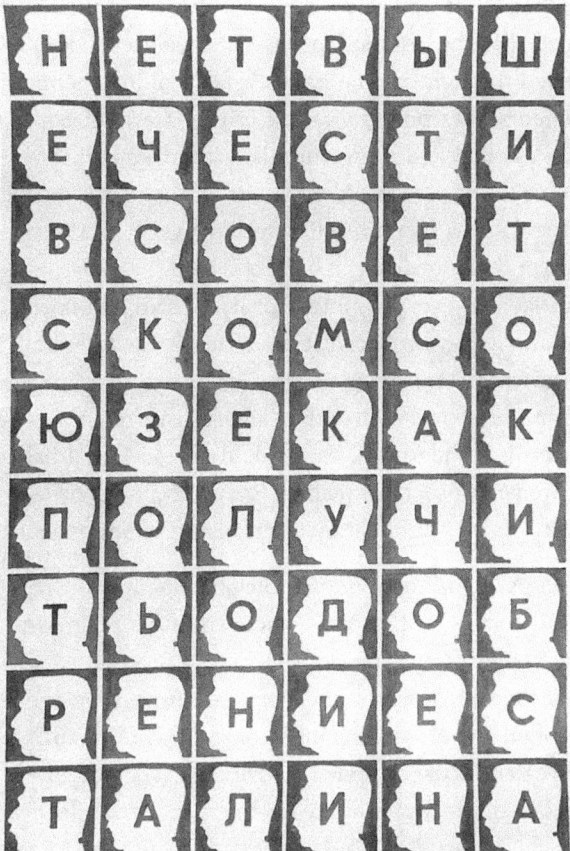

FIG. 4.2
Vyacheslav
Akhunov, *ABC*
(The Alphabet of
Totalitarianism)
(There is no higher
honor in the Soviet
Union than to
receive an approval
from Stalin). 1976.
Paper, watercolor,
61 cm × 39 cm.
Courtesy of the
artist.

with "modernism" very well. But it was enough to remember Kazimir Malevich's work *The Red Horsemen* or [Vladimir] Tatlin's *Tower* as the premises for the emergence of the socialist modernism. Undoubtedly it was all about de-ideologization (deconceptualization) of everything that was considered in the USSR to be sacred, untouchable, pertaining to the party and the ruling ideology. It became necessary to reform the very nature of Socialist realism and its practices, to work for the emergence in the Soviet art of a new type of artistic experience and thinking.

Back in the '70s, I imagined socialist modernism as an overcoming of the Soviet ideological limitations in art. I saw it as a trend which borrowed the Western artistic languages and techniques in combination with socialist realism. Socialist modernism could adopt what was created by the socialist realists, but changes the accents and the ideological contexts, removing the basis of the communist ideology. I assumed that the artistic language of socialist modernism would be shaped through commentaries, analytical judgments, paradoxical statements, interpretations, and critical views of both the socialist realist method and the modernist art movements. Socialist modernism could be a reconsideration of all the established norms of socialist realism. It was a reaction to the present situation in socialist realism and modernism, in both of which there was no space for any innovation—everything that could be said had been already expressed and archived. Socialist modernism was to erode the boundaries between the hostile ideologies of the two struggling political and economic systems, each with its own artistic territories and languages. Socialist modernism, then could become the final stage in the development of socialist realism in the form of its negation and a possibility for the continuation of the history of Soviet art.

TLOSTANOVA: What is in your opinion the role of contemporary art in building the civil society in the post-Soviet repressive regimes? When any adequate opposition to power is lacking, when the social theoretical models tend to be weak and borrowed from someone else's sources (as coloniality of thinking infects social theorists much more than artists), can an artist or some creative activist community play any visible political role and produce any meanings and affects emancipating our consciousness? Could they perhaps use the fact that any artistic utterance is metaphorical by definition and hence is able to quickly and more accurately grasp the Zeitgeist, the change of the imaginary, and is still able to escape from censorship? In what forms can art more effectively exist today as a political utterance?

AKHUNOV: If we look at the emergence of contemporary art in Uzbekistan and wider, in the post-Soviet Central Asia, we would have to admit that it is almost nonexistent. The first Uzbek exhibition of contemporary art opened in 2005. It was called *Constellation* and organized with the financial support of the Swiss Bureau for the Collaboration in Culture and Art. The exhibition was closed three days after the opening. The same year they closed the public nongovernmental Center for the New Art that I officially founded two years before. In 2010 the group of young Uzbek artists who were my pupils and used to regularly come to my workshop, were called to their respective bosses and warned by the unknown people that Akhunov is an American spy and if they were to be seen again next to me they would lose their job and would never find another one. They had to make their choice.

On my initiative a group of young, enthusiastic students conducted a poll at the Uzbek National Art Institute. The future artists and the young graduates of the same institute between eighteen and twenty-five years of age were asked what part was played by the contemporary art in the life of our country and if it could act as a catalyst, contributing to the development of the post-Soviet Uzbek society. The results of this poll were published in the book *Winter: Poetics and Politics* (Vishmidt et al. 2013), which was a part of the Central Asian pavilion project at the 55th Venice Biennale. The answers were predictable, yet still quite shocking.

1. Art is:
   (a) Art for art's sake—a creative experiment and a discovery of the new artistic forms.
   50%—yes, 50%—no
   (b) A commercial endeavor whose goal is to sell the artistic product.
   80%—yes, 20%—no
   (c) A social-political movement with the artist as an activist whose goal is revolutionary changes and overcoming of social alienation.
   10%—yes, 90%—no
2. Does the contemporary art of Uzbekistan meet your expectations?
   10%—yes, 90%—no
3. Have you ever encountered at exhibitions works by Uzbek artists that reflect social and political themes?
   100%—no
4. Is it necessary to introduce the history of modernism into art college curricula?
   40%—yes, 60%—no
5. Should teachers at art schools and colleges warn their students against any penchant for contemporary art, thus causing them to have negative opinions of this art?
   50%—yes, 50%—no

6. Does Uzbek art need private galleries independent from the state?

40%—yes, 60%—no

At the same time, the state holds the International Biennial of Contemporary Art in Tashkent. Yet we have no private, independent or state galleries which would specialize in the representation and promotion of contemporary art and would be interested in the training of specialists in this area. The local organizers of the large projects often have no idea of the processes taking place in contemporary art which means that there are still no premises for organizing any large events such as international artistic forums. All of the previous biennials of contemporary art in Tashkent had been just a formality as the regime appointed its art bureaucrats to the key positions and they acted as censors immediately banning all critical works. It is not even the question of wasting the state budget, but more the unbelievable unprofessionalism and lack of adequate specialists in the area of large international art projects and most importantly, the total ideological control of the state.

The bureaucrats do not care why there is no dialogue between our local artists and the latest trends in contemporary art worldwide, or how one looks for new artistic languages. Due to the curators' low professionalism, any communication turns out to be a mere semblance and, as a result, a failure. There are no curatorial strategies; the curators are not able to clearly formulate any original ideas. It would be interesting to create each time a new exhibition structure and elaborate a new tactic, making it possible to improvise and overcome the narrow disciplinary barriers and take into account the historical and cultural conditions of our country. The local would-be curators are only schematically copying illustrations from the catalogues, journals and internet sites of the existing international forums to which they have never been invited and hence could not possibly gain any first-hand experience. In the end the imitation of knowledge and experience leads to a parody instead of a wholesome and successful major Central Asian international art forum. The lack of professionalism on the curators' part does not bother the bureaucrats who take the final decision on the organization of such projects. They do not care if it were a real art event or a low quality simulation. What they do care about is that under their wise supervision one more contemporary art forum took place, the prizes were quietly and eventlessly awarded, the guests were massively *chapan*ized and taken sightseeing in Samarkand,[2] the organizers praised themselves in the local media and now can safely report to their bosses that it was a successful event.

Often artists complain about persecutions of any independent initiatives by the authorities who fear the artists' unorthodox interpretations opposed to the official legitimized line in art and in politics. Yet, paradoxically, these artists almost never attempt to do an independent work. They complain about financial difficulties, bans and consequently, their worry of being left with no sustenance, their fear for their own and their family's lives and well-being. Such arguments are grounded in fear—a fear of being repressed! At the same time these same people are ready to be commissioned to do the poorly paid ideological state works risking to be mocked by censors, artistic unions and bureaucrats.

It means that after gaining independence the country still recreates the same politics of violence and suppression which Moscow successfully used in relation to its colonial peripheries. But today it is the local political elite which uses the same methods of colonial violence against any efforts at liberalization of our society. Let us call it an internal colonization. The authoritarian power is a pack of internal colonizers who are profiting from the peoples' ignorance and especially their ignorance of liberal values. Consequently, all the efforts to legitimize the real contemporary art are always nipped in the bud. Historically Tashkent has never had any underground or other forms of protest art such as mobile artistic communities, and anyone involved in art sphere is scared to death to be persecuted by the state.

As for creative forms of contemporary art as a political utterance, I would assume that any forms would do if interesting and creative ideas are put in their basis, if they use an unusual optic and develop unconventional interpretations. Yet the most effective, topical and adamant of all genres for me are performance, actionism, happening, which include the whole specter of multidisciplinary actions (music, fiction, poetry, theater, cinema, video, dance, declamation, etcetera), in short, the art of action.

TLOSTANOVA: Your artwork has long been known and appreciated in the world. Your works are exhibited in the West and in the East at the most prestigious professional forums. And this is wonderful that you are appreciated even if sometimes you cannot even attend your own exhibitions because you are not granted an exit visa from Uzbekistan. Yet a number of artists from the post-Soviet space and particularly those from the Caucasus and Central Asia experience some Orientalist déjà vue, which is expressed in the exoticization and commercialization of their art and of themselves as some neocolonial goods in the context of contemporary global art. Do you feel these negative sides of the global recognition? Or you have your own recipe of how to avoid it?

AKHUNOV: The "Socialist" was crossed out from the formula "Socialist in its content, national in its form" and "capitalist" was put instead. It is not only art products, but also purely commercial goods that are often represented in national exotic garbs as playing the Orient. There is a simple goal behind it—to identify ourselves in the midst of mediocre art products as being different and therefore, to attract attention to what we are doing and to sell our works. It is no longer an appropriation or a repetition as such, but rather an exotic national wrap into which the replications of Western works are often packaged. Usually it is stressed that we are able to make everything just like the Westerners do. Often when the Western grants stop to be poured into the post-Soviet republics, the artists' initiative also dries out, and it becomes impossible to find anyone working in contemporary art, as it happened in Kazakhstan. International art forums, which for a long time have acted as centers and targets of art-nomadism and as a part of the global tourist business, let the world discover the unknown exotic varieties of contemporary art from the Third World countries.

In 2007 in London I conducted a number of actions around the question of why the artists from the Third World are confined to the role of props or exotic exhibits which must serve as a garnish to the programs created by the artists from the developed countries. I was cleaning with a toothbrush and shampoo, the tiles of the yard of the Royal Academy of Arts and the work of German artist Kiffer exhibited in that yard, the columns and stairs of the National Art Museum and the lions at the Trafalgar Square, the metal details and the décor of the royal palace, the stairs of the old and new Tate Gallery buildings, and even the stuffed animals at private apartments (*Cleaner*, 2007).

The feeling of being fastened to this or that exhibition as an exotic object was persisting until the Istanbul biennial of 2009 where they exhibited seven of my projects consisting of over eighty works. Only the dead artists are usually honored that way. After Istanbul there was a number of serious exhibitions, several museums bought my works and as a result, I was invited to take part in the famous Documenta 13 in Kassel, in exhibitions at the New Museum in New York, in the Pompidou Centre in Paris and at the Queen Sofia Museum in Madrid.

But why is it so? The reason for my recognition is that I work with the Soviet identity in continuation of my series from the nineteen seventies and within socialist modernism that we discussed earlier. This refers to the *Red Mantras of the USSR*, *The Red Party Line*, to my *Leniniana*, the *Art-Cheology of the USSR*, to the *Doubt, Procrustean Bed of Marxism-Leninism* and a dozen others. The artistic foundations were laid in the legendary times. Still, I had to prove my professional suitability anew by means of my contemporary projects.

Today I can choose my projects according to the "under doubt" principle. To put something under doubt means to discuss the alarming sense of historical repetition and insularity, the historical vacuum marked by a lack of events, by stagnation, and also, to reflect on my own works, my own feelings that I put under doubt. In the conditions of exhausted forms which have led to the impossibility of re-inscribing the signs (as new forms), the very doubt as a medium of all other mediums is doubted. Maybe this is my recipe to avoid the negative sides of the global recognition: to put everything which used to happen and which is going on now, and first of all, to put myself and my existence, under scrutiny. To doubt everything I do. My personal exhibition, which is now in the making will be curated by Viktor Misiano (who will also write one of the catalogue texts along with Boris Groys) and will be called "Under Doubt."[3]

TLOSTANOVA: A quarter of a century has passed after the collapse of the USSR and there is an opinion that the Soviet legacy is already over and it is time to museumize it even for those of us who were shaped within its tight embrace and often in spite of it. On the other hand, the lacking self-reflection, the missing repentance or any work with cultural and historical complexes, traumas and memories, leads to a never ending wandering in circles, to falling over into the same

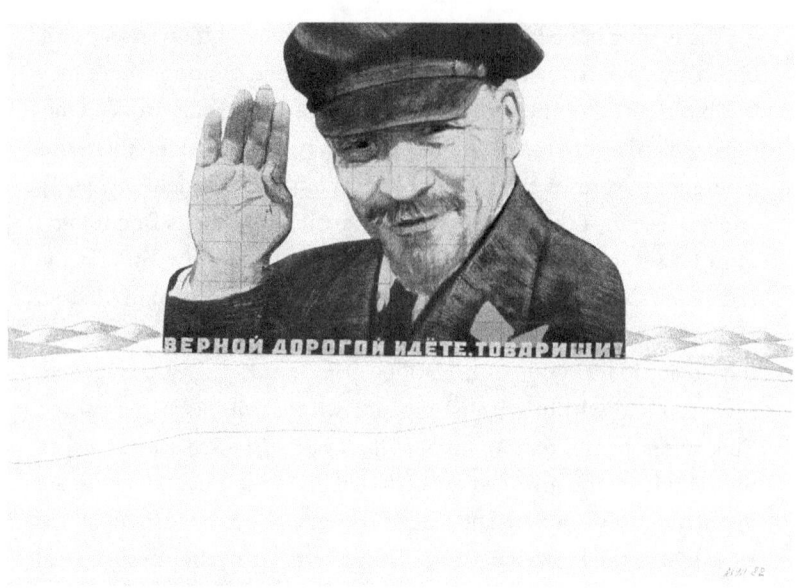

FIG. 4.3 Vyacheslav Akhunov, *You Are Following the Correct Road, Comrades* (Lenin's plan of monumental propaganda). 1982. Paper, serial print, pencil, 40 cm × 29.5 cm. From the *Desert of Oblivion* series. Courtesy of the artist.

trap again and again, to a revival of the most dangerous imperial/ Soviet *ressentiment,* for instance, in Russia. How has the trajectory of your own artistic priorities, interests, and leitmotivs changed in the last twenty-five years? What have you lost and gained as an artist? What do you find important today and tomorrow?

AKHUNOV: Igor Savitsky acquired forty five of my works—two canvases and some graphics, for his famous collection in Nukus.[4] This happened in the fall of 1980 about a year after I graduated from the Surikov State Academic Institute. In 1977 the Tretyakov gallery bought four of my canvases for its collection. In 1989 after my trip to the United States and visits of many contemporary art museums, I told myself: "Everything has been already discovered, everything has been done before me." I had not realized then that I was doing something important, unique and unlike anyone else, that somehow I managed to rethink the modernist discourse and formulate my own understanding of what I was doing and what other nonconformist artists in the USSR were also doing then—socialist modernism. For me, the struggle with the regime was taking a playful form. I did it with the help of art, but it was a dangerous and even deadly game, I was interrogated by the KGB and my life was under constant surveillance.

After *perestroika*, when the bans were lifted and the empire collapsed I lost any interest in the game and in 1990 I packed all my works into boxes and suitcases and shelved them for twenty years. Instead of that I started working in the cinema and attempted to learn how to make video art. I worked with film director Ali Khamrayev on the films *Tamerlane* and *Chenghis Khan* at an Italian cinema company, I visited Cinecittà Studios in Rome, Mosfilm, Sverdlovsk Cinema Company. I spent some time in Germany, England, and other places in Europe—in short, I was learning and working. My first three video art works were demonstrated publicly at the Tashkent exhibition *Constellation* in 2005. But before that there were several unofficial apartment screenings and experiments, efforts to assemble the video materials with the use of two video recorders, conceptual drawing series, inspired by the 1970s–80s works of Nam June Paik. Simultaneously, I started writing fiction texts more consistently than before. I worked on scripts, novels, and even poems. I have written two novels—*The Foundling* and the *Uzbek Transit* about the life of guest workers. Generally, I was engaged in things that had nothing to do with paints, varnish and thinners until I heard of contemporary art movements in Kazakhstan and Kirghizia. In the late 1990s I realized that the Uzbek society was in a worse situation than in the USSR and my interest in the game whose rules were becoming stricter every year, was revived.

In 2000 I was invited to take part in the first Central Asian festival of contemporary art in Almaty, but I have participated in contemporary art forums in the Soviet years as well. For instance, I took part in the Asian Art Biennale Bangladesh in 1987, where I won a prize. In Almaty together with the felt artist Burbukan Borubayeva (Bishkek), we made a sixteen meter installation based on my design. It was made of felt, sand and clay and called *The Desert of Oblivion. Quicksand*. The work was awarded a grand prix at the festival, and this is how I came back to contemporary art.

To share my experience with younger artists I initiated an officially registered nongovernmental Center for the New Art. Visual-plastic anthropology. In two years the National Security Service closed it as a hostile to the state line in the arts.

The 1970s–80s for me were a period of total isolation, mostly underground, hermetic, with a theoretical bent. There were simply no nonconformist artists, writers or film directors in Central Asia. The second period starting from the late 1990s and until now can be defined as an implementation of my theoretical ideas into practice. I mean my theoretical experience of a multimedia artist of the eighties that I managed to transfer in the nineties into the practical sphere, when I had a chance to make installations, video art, performances, actions, sculptures, and photo-projects, focusing on the social and political problems and actively criticizing the regime. In a way, I was the pioneer of multimedia art in Central Asia and Uzbekistan. Besides, in the local art situation, I was the founder and popularizer of contemporary art and it is first of all as an artist that I managed to gain at least some personal freedom in this deadening totalitarian state. When the curators of the Istanbul Biennial of Contemporary Art came to Tashkent in 2009, my suitcases were reopened and the archives were finally shown. Immediately after that I was invited to display my works in Berlin, in Tanas gallery and at the Istanbul Biennial where my success was celebrated by the exiled Uzbek political opposition presided by Muhammad Salikh.[5] After that encounter I was always rejected the exit visas whenever I applied for one. I have become a hostage.

Today, tomorrow as well as yesterday it has been always important for me to remain in the interstice. On the one hand, it allows seeing the pragmatics of the demonized technological process of the attraction art époque which is oriented toward the consumers' mass tastes when technologies usurp the space of the transcendental subject and the human being is replaced with its technological double. Then a realistic depiction (let us say of a flower) is mingling and hybridizing with a computer interface, a multimedia frame, or a technological process. On the other hand, we deal with the all-encompassing representation of the nonaccountable appropriation and the simulative devices of the distorted representation of reality borrowed from mass-media, the domination of simulacra, the advertising commercial tricks and the political engagement of art. In the narrow interstice between these two extremes the social and political art and the topical culture exist. And the interstice lets in only the initiated ones. For others the place is at the extremes.

CHAPTER FIVE

Reflecting on Time, Space,
and Memory with Afanassy Mamedov

Afanassy Mamedov is one of the very few Russophone writers who fully
embody the postcolonial and the postsocialist human condition. The intersection of postcolonialism and postsocialism has not yet received any
serious critical reflection in Russia and is not even admitted to be a le-
gitimate topic of discourse by the majority of the critical establishment.
They often assume that both postcolonial and postsocialist studies are
imported and imposed from abroad. Mamedov has Azeri and Jewish
roots. Born in Baku, the capital of Soviet Azerbaijan, Mamedov moved to
Moscow as a young man. As a successful journalist and winner of many
Russian literary prizes, as well as an editor of the Jewish journal *L'chaim*,
Mamedov is one of the very few contemporary authors writing in Russian
whose prose is attuned to the global tendencies of transculturation, cultural and linguistic creolization, playful negotiation of the global and the
local, trickster-shifting identifications, and nostalgic spatial memories of
non-Russian post-Soviet multicultural cities. What follows is an excerpt
from a longer interview I conducted with Mamedov on the nature of

fiction and on the post-Soviet unhomed writers who infinitely linger between various worlds and times.

MADINA TLOSTANOVA: I first got acquainted with your work in 2000. And since then for me the most interesting aspect of your fiction has been the embodiment of transcultural space in your texts, how it on the one hand, expresses the picturesque and palpable materiality of this world and on the other, acts as a reservoir of many histories. In my view, space in your works, often takes over time, space conquers time. Similar things happen in the famous Southern novel in the United States (Faulkner and Carson McCullers among others), as well as in a number of postcolonial works, such as Salman Rushdie's and V. S. Naipaul's. But you have your own always recognizable way of representing spatial histories. How would you define the sense of place in fiction in general and in your own works? Does the recipe of spatial-temporal correlation and interaction change from one work to another?

AFANASSY MAMEDOV: Yes and no. The basis/carcass remains the same or almost the same. It all depends on how much you change yourself. Alexander Blok said that the author's style is a constant, invariable dimension because in order to change his style the author himself would have to alter completely. Otherwise, it is not a style but just a simulation. I have trusted Blok for many years, yet today I am almost sure that any author can change beyond recognition two or three times in his life. And the "sense of place," the "played out past" together with the "open space" of the future, play an important role in this uncontrollable process.

The sense of place depends on preferences, on what are we dreaming about and how deep was our sleep when we woke up . . . No matter how we cut our routes, no matter how we hurry up or slow down, we always arrive at the same time and at the same point with all our characters. They are also, by the way, subject to changes, provided that their emergence in our text was determined not only by the main story line but also by the suggestiveness of the text.

You know, it often seems to us that we, the writers, are smarter than the text, written and published, but it is not always so. It often happens that the resulting text turns out to be much cleverer, much more significant and wonderful than its authors, and this paradoxical divergence may last for years. It refers particularly to those writers who create their texts in the conditions of partial or complete liberation from the moment of cognition, to use a Zen-Buddhist metaphor. I think that my characteristic style is connected not as much with the quest for such a style or its conscious building (I am always catching up with my own texts), as with my place of birth—Baku, Second Parallel Street 20/67, apartment 37, and with my date of birth—1960, the time of the thaw, and with the family—a Jewish Azeri family, with its own multilayered history. . . .

I am not the first scriptor/writer in this family. A partiality to writing sat deeply in our genes, but also the karmic debt of my grandfather and father and other writing relatives that I inherited. All of this was not defining until the moment when I defined myself. My choice depended on many things, including the endless series of hobbies. They shaped me as a person of the Abrahamic triangle with some Zen elements.

It is easier for me to answer your question if I tell you about my literary preferences. When I was young in contrast with my peers who were keen on fantasy, mystery stories, historical and adventure novels I read a lot of "boring" Russian classical literature. And from very early on looked at the Caucasus, where I was born and grew up with the eyes of a "colonist," "someone who arrived from elsewhere." Ideally, this look was from above, except for the fact that it was fake, it was a mask. And this prevented me from properly taking off. Later the mask became my second nature and I started to finally climb, but that happened already in Moscow.

TLOSTANOVA: When did you move to Moscow? What were the reasons for your departure?

MAMEDOV: I left for Moscow in 1985 for many reasons, most of which can be described as personal. But then it seemed to me that I simply outgrew my city. I was protecting myself from the miseries of life with the help of the symbolists and the Russian Silver age literature. I was saving myself with Nabokov's and Gazdanov's prose. In the Russian literature divided after the October revolt I definitely preferred the immigrant part. It was so full of tension, drama, apocalyptic experience which none of the other national literatures can offer, in my view. The Literary Institute[1] also played an important part in shaping me as an individual and as an artist. The 1990s were not just the years of freedom; we tested our strength with this freedom.

TLOSTANOVA: Twentieth-century writers from countries and regions which went through the traumatic experience of wars, genocide, exile, colonization, dictatorship, totalitarian regimes, have developed in response particular recurrent and recognizable aesthetic and poetological forms, genres, and devices. This is how the Eastern European protest fiction emerged, the German tradition of reckoning with the past after World War II, the post-dictatorship fiction in a number of Latin American countries and certainly the postcolonial novel as an international phenomenon. Yet it seems that the postsocialist space has not managed in the last twenty five years (since the collapse of the USSR) to come up with its own model or even realize its own difference in poetics, in the set of devices, and the optics for seeing the world. It does not mean of course that all of these elements do not exist. It is just that they exist in some not entirely reflected upon, not fully realized form. And part of the reason, as I see it, is the unwillingness of the rest of the world and its aesthetic establishment to admit the presence of such a distinct post-Soviet model of fiction and art. The only works that have found a mass recognition in the rest of the world are the straightforward political illustrations and commercialized nostalgia. Is there such a thing as post-Soviet fiction, in your opinion, as a separate school, modality or genre? Does it have a future or it is going to disappear or become something else very soon?

MAMEDOV: Post-Soviet fiction definitely does not exist as a school or as a trend. I agree with you here. As a modality, it does not exist either it seems. We used to be a country of fresh newspapers, and now we are a country of fresh books. Our literature is most probably a literature of islands in the sea, which does not make it less valuable by the way. Why is it so? I think there are no leaders left in this fiction. No irrefutable leaders. And those who used to be or are assigned to be leaders, usually from above, and by those publishers who publish these writers "a novel a year." These are big publishers who are certain that the trouble-proof functioning of their business can indeed influence the literary processes, because for the bosses contemporary literature is a process and a quite controllable process at that (business, nothing personal). But they forget one Taoist truth: "Things often grow when someone is trying to diminish them and shrink when someone attempts to exalt them." This works for people as well. Another important thing is how our selected intelligentsia behaved after 1991. What the KGB has not managed to do was done by the ordinary snickers bar . . . In short, the writers swallowed the bait of the Western material abundance . . .

It is possible that for the post-Soviet fiction to become a school and a modality, as we would like it to happen, what is needed is a cumbersome political event, some important milestone, a mark in the history of our country. Maybe we are coming closer to such an event now, I mean what is happening in the world and what position Russia has taken in relation to the West.

You ask if the post-Soviet fiction is going to dissolve with time. I do not think so. We have no choice, we cannot juxtapose to it, so to say, an unofficial post-Soviet literature, because in the last years we have not managed to create such a counter-cultural phenomenon, there was simply no need for it. No one was banned; everyone who wanted to be heard—from here and from there—could be published. Can it become different? When it happens the post-Soviet fiction will stop being itself, which maybe both of us will celebrate. Because at the moment when it happens, a real post-Soviet fiction would emerge instead of a clumsy corporate product in the troubled minds of always hurrying literary critics. And then it will be possible to study it and find its leaders asking the question of who should be allowed in this literature and who should be left out.

But I am really answering your question from the end, it would be more appropriate to start from the fact that it is necessary to define the temporal frames without which we will not understand what is included into the concept of post-Soviet literature. It would be convenient to think that it starts after the collapse of the USSR, but I think that the count should begin two-three years before. I would offer 1989 as the starting date. And also I would not wait until this fiction dies in agony and would sentence it to its end before. I believe that it happened in 2003–2004. After that a different sort of fiction emerges which you have just mentioned. But many people simply did not notice its originating moment. This means that the temporal frame of the post-Soviet fiction has been just the past ten or twelve years, and maybe even less.

Now when we have defined the temporal frames we should think of what authors we could include—all those writing in Russian in different parts of the world, or only Russian Federation, or the Commonwealth of Independent States? If we are stricter about the term "post-Soviet," then we should include only the authors who used to live and write in the ex-Soviet space, but I would shun from this. In any case this is none of my business to decide whom to let in and whom to throw out, whom to call a general, and whom to bury in a mass grave as a brave lance-corporal. This is the task of independent experts and they are to decide. I feel somehow the imperfection of the concept "post-Soviet fiction" which used to be convenient up to a certain moment.

TLOSTANOVA: Many of your readers are attracted, even mesmerized, with the images of Baku and Moscow, of many foreign towns and cities which you visited and whose spirit you are subtly recreating, for example, in the fragmentary *Absheron Chronicles*—a book quite unconventional in the genre and narrative sense. In fiction space, and especially urban space which is highly man-made, is entirely unreal, utterly subjective; it capriciously changes under the influence of our moods and our wishes, but also has its own will and nature. When a writer comes into such a space and starts playing with topos (from Greek τόπος—space as location), strange things happen. I could not help feeling that your spatial portraits are not photographs, not documents, but rather paintings, so to say, that is a highly imagined topos of Baku, Moscow, Istanbul, Germany, or the Maghreb. Gradually from work to work there emerges a complex community of characters, families, friends migrating from one story or novel to another. It is a certain saga not unlike Faulkner's Yoknapatawpha—with its own carefully striated and lovingly mapped world, so deceivingly real and at the same time, imagined. What is the recipe of such an artistic reality? How real or imagined is it? Or maybe similarly to Vladimir Nabokov, you do not believe in reality without quotation marks and you add into your texts only the very necessary modicum of such mediocre reality in order to fool the reader who is looking for realism and plausibility? Such a hapless reader will encounter in the pages of your books the real streets, places, and names—Shemakhinka, Parallel streets,

Seaside Boulevard, Tverskaya street with many side streets around the Patriarch Ponds in Moscow. But all of these are stylized spaces, the optics of their representation is recognizably yours and they are always marked with a spatial confusion, a phantasmagoric trace, an element of detachment and estrangement making the familiar look unpredictable. Already in your first works I was stricken by this hybridity, this overlapping of different spaces, this very specific depth. And now it seems that this element has intensified.

More and more often spaces become openly fantastic, mystical and esoteric as in a number of your recent works populated by trickster characters who are undergoing various metamorphoses. What sort of signs are those? Can we interpret them as an impossibility of finding a way out in this world? Or is it a peculiar version of the old Bakhtin's road chronotope which we find in the medieval romance and in the picaresque novel? In your case the road chronotope was first realized as nostalgia for Baku and the adventures of a stranger in Moscow. But now more and more often it is a path through the looking glass, into other realities, into the twilight esoteric worlds, into yoga and martial arts as a philosophy of life. Why such a shift?

MAMEDOV: I am glad you remembered the *Absheron Chronicles*. It is a border work; it sort of ends a long period in my life. It sums up the époque of *Frau Shram*. I was writing that novel in the state of being open to all winds and I did not care about anyone's opinion, but the *Absheron Chronicles* is a hermetic work even if it seems to be light and readable. Working on it, I always kept in mind what would people think of me. There are certain moments in life when your youth turns out to be wiser and brighter than "the age of wisdom." What made you ask about the esoteric and yoga worlds is probably the triptych "When fire keeps water" and especially its last novelette "*Nargiz and Aramis*." This work is in many ways a test, I had to see if I really can let the other reality into my/our world, if these two worlds can coexist in my prose, what language should I use in certain narrative moments, when both worlds are indistinguishable and one of them overlaps with the other . . . This triptych was the foothold for the short novel I am finishing now.[2] There are great masters of such prose from Kafka to Bulgakov; I needed to see if I can enter this literary territory, this literary regiment with my own face, what would be the losses, if any. I could have written such prose earlier, but I felt before that I have no right to do it and then, I very much nurtured a healthy man in myself, a man firmly standing with his feet on the ground and pretending that an "other reality" maybe exists, but is none of my care. But as soon as this ground slipped from under my feet I felt an urge to write differently, I got a feeling that I acquired that right.

My writing is connected with the road I once chose. This road as it turns out, is linked with Buddhism, but not with traditional varieties such as ashrams, Indian, Chinese, Japanese, or Tibetan and not even with the Buddhism processed by Albert Schweitzer or Teitaro Suzuki, but rather with that Eastern fairy tale which Westerners invented for themselves. First of all I mean Salinger's and Hesse's Buddhism. For them it was also a state of their soul, a longing for light, an immediate and inexpressible state which is necessary to fix to be able to come back to it and use it properly to save oneself. In this sense there is not much difference between the core Buddhism and the ashram. Maybe I am wrong, let us say, this is my feeling. I do not want to touch upon theoretical or technical aspects, such as, for example, what is a halt in a dialogue and how does it affect a soul prepared or not prepared by Buddhism. Let us agree that our Buddhism is the Buddhism of intellectuals and artists. You stepped out to the balcony to have a smoke and have a cup of tea and found yourself in a different century or millennium, or even in a different dimension, you understood something and got back with no losses and this is already good.

But if on top of that you carefully extinguished your cigarette and washed your cup without pushing anyone with your elbow or making their life difficult with your cigarette smoke, then you are a hero, then you understand what is Zen. The change of course was not induced by me. I would feel much more comfortable living the way I lived and writing the way I wrote before. But certain things happen independently of our wishes, let us call them the twists of fate. They are such "Finnegan's wakes." Good if you can disappear, hide in some sabbatical. As a rule, there is no point in clinging to the past. You can only hope for some assistance from the outside . . .

As for the real and imagined in my prose, I invent only those things that—as Sergei Dovlatov would say—imbue the narrative reality with some degree of probability, everything else is redundant. So it is not really a question of composition or form . . . I offered a sacrifice if you wish and now I am responsible for it in my writings, and the rest of it is not mine, I leave it to others with no regret. You said it very well and to the point when you mentioned reality in quotation marks. Someone else's experience is this reality in inverted commas; one can remove the commas only when it becomes one's own experience. Initiation is, in fact, removing the quotation marks from reality, and not just removing but also rocking this reality which may be dangerous at times. And maybe that is why one cannot be initiated at one's own will but only at the will of heaven, if you excuse my pathetic tone. Maybe this is why real literature has never heard of such bodies as the Ministry of Culture and does not know anything about such mind-widening books as *The 100 Best Contemporary Authors*.

TLOSTANOVA: You always create a second reality existing entirely in your mind and in your whimsical memory. And it is about memory that I would like to ask you. Literature as well as cinema is certainly the art of memory. But its role can be quite different. What is it in your case? Is it a conservation of the past, nostalgia for the childhood or an exorcism as an effort to get rid of the previous experience, including the Soviet one?

MAMEDOV: I think all of what you enumerated exists, but the question is which of them dominates. I feel that I am the least preoccupied with the liberation from the Soviet experience, if I understood you correctly, and you implied here a political alignment affecting our generation. You see, I have always been rather apolitical and now even more so—long live Fellini! And it will not be possible to divide the purely Soviet from the post-Soviet, well, maybe only the lemonade and caviar from the Sebastopol sparkling wine.

Indeed, I stopped conserving the past or being nostalgic about my childhood. Flash-backs become less and less important in my writing. You are right, without the art of memory there is no art as such. The question is what do you want to remember as an artist and as an ordinary human being, how the former and the latter are positioned inside yourself. It would be wonderful to get rid of the previous experience, especially if it were negative, but one has to be very careful here because in the heat of liberation it is easy not to notice that you started to liberate yourself from yourself. Not everyone and not always is fit for Castaneda style cleanings. The human being is very fragile, one cannot stop respecting oneself, or start refusing a mission one was assigned, generally, or in a concrete period of one's life—just because one is tired or sick with it and wants to jump over several steps in one's subconscious. . . . If God needs to set you free of some negative experience he would do it and it is not your task to decide when. All you can do is to pour out some water from the overflowing glass. I think when I am writing this is exactly what I am doing. Maybe this is the main reason . . .

TLOSTANOVA: The space we have been discussing so far is also a home, a certain anchor of the soul as Salman Rushdie once said. Yet when there is no real, stable home—and in today's world, there are more and more people who are in such an unhomed situation—its role can be performed by language. Let us talk a bit about the role of language/languages in your works. What is the specificity of language in contemporary Russophone literature written by multicultural authors from the postsoviet space? I feel that so far their works often fall out of the critics' tunnel vision or are distorted in accordance with some moth-eaten Soviet formulas of the national in its form and Socialist in its content (today it simply becomes just Russian instead of Soviet). It is much more convenient to label the author as a "singer" of his native Abkhazia who grew up feeding on the great Russian culture, even if he does not glorify his native land, experiencing a complex love-hate relationship with it instead. It is easier to call a writer, for example, a "Russophone Kabardin author" (this is how I was called by one of the label-loving literary critics). But these labels are a fake. How would you define your works in this sense?

It seems that language is yet another touchstone in the process of the post-Soviet writers' entering the larger world of global fiction. There are almost no translations or it is a predicable set of figures representing Russian fiction abroad. Moreover, translations are often inadequate because multilingualism and multiculturalism are barely possible to translate. Literature in this sense is an inconvenient and almost archaic genre in today's rapidly visualizing world. It is not dancing, not painting, not installation or clownery. In literature words still rule. And this immediately problematizes any translation between cultures, between the worlds of values even in the post-Soviet space itself. Are your multilingualism and chorus narration translatable from one Russian into another? What is your attitude to Russian language as a writer's tool?

MAMEDOV: Language as home?! It is an unexpected comparison . . . I would agree with you, if we add the adjective "ancestral." But then we would have to speak about those changes that took place in the last quarter of a century in the yard of our civilization. Today we will not find laundry drying on the clothesline, or cats sunbathing on the roof of the communal lavatory and the mechanical doorbells went out of fashion. Not only these, but many other things, comprise the idea of our ancestral home. I cannot tell you when and why these homes derailed, but I am certain that they were a crucial part of our postcaveman civilization.

Contemporary people have forgotten what their ancestral home is. In a sense this makes them cut off from their childhood, for our ancestral home is that very shell in which our material and spiritual bodies were carefully nurtured. It is not only the language we were going to use when communicating with others, but also the language which we learned to use when speaking with ourselves, the language of our metaphysical self or the language to which we entrust ourselves for the rest of our life. Your ancestral home is also your first library, the literal link with ancestors who lived and died in these walls, and the seven drafts and the first dreams and everything else without which literature and art would maybe survive but become mediocre and middlebrow. One can move to another continent, but when one knows that somewhere there is this ancestral home, one still lives and sees the world in a particular way. The book indeed stopped to play the role it used to play only recently. There is no home as a home and no library as a library anymore. The book is sent into a cloud storage or a memory-stick.

Our language could not help changing with the emergence of internet and social media . . . There is less and less need for the richness of language, while its development and mastering require too much time and effort. And it is not practical. Then it is better to master other languages. We need a second and third language to get more information and share it with our "friends," without experiencing any linguistic barrier while travelling, feeling ourselves protected. The language of contemporary literature consists of a number of linguistic clichés and formulas at best. I would call them the ribs of language.

And it happens not because everyone has suddenly become ardent adherents of linguistic norms and wants to report their work to philologists who would in their turn hasten to correct all the mistakes. It is just that souls are more and more fading out. And this is the cradle of all literary trash.

You are right that literature has become outdated in today's quickly visualizing world. I think that cinema, painting, and plastic arts have also been challenged, but in a less serious way. Yet they will not escape this fate with time. Our eye is also an instrument, directly linked with our intellect and soul . . . Simplification and flattening refer to contemporary translations as well. People who speak fluent English may easily not know who is Philip Sidney or Ben Johnson. They may not know who John Donne is. But I am sure they will easily find their way to Heathrow airport. Important cultural codes and keys are being lost . . . No matter how ingenious the translation is, it cannot possibly recreate all the subtleties of the original, it can only give us a bunch of keys. The rest depends on the reader.

Several times there were preparations to translate my prose into German and Turkish. They say there are even some drafts of translations of my stories. I take it calmly. I am not sure at all that my works could be translated at least on any acceptable level. For this to happen, it is necessary that the translator knows Russian literature and culture very well, as well as Russian colloquial and literary language and, most importantly, is really keen on the author he is going to translate. This is the minimum. And I am not sure that anyone anywhere is so feverish about my prose . . . I do not need just some translations. I can live without them.

I discovered my language by chance. Sometime in the late 1980s, I was listening to Radio Freedom. In some cultural program they were discussing a prize-winning novel by a Corsican writer delivered in non-normative French. The custodians of the purity of the French language were enraged whereas the readers loved the book. Then I understood the legitimacy of my Russian, not the one I was learning at school, and not the one I am speaking in Moscow or am trying to write in now, but the one which was spoken in Baku, by the whole street or just the inhabitants of our yard, the Russian that was spoken by the Bakinian Spring. And after this random discovery I wrote "Weddings" and they then pulled all other works.

"Weddings" was the first short-story noticed by the critics. Inspired by the literary bureaucrats they attempted to send me to the division of national authors. This was probably easier and safer for them—the critics are dependent people after all. But I refused this offer and pretended that I did not hear it. And of course I found myself outside of the national mainstream. Judging by the fact that many years have passed since then and each of us was left with what we have and what we are, I think that such a state of affairs is convenient for both me and those who control our contemporary literature. But I would not like for my words to be interpreted as some accusation. Let us finish with a Latin saying *Suum cuique* [May all get their due]. May this overused Latin truth resonate once again. Especially that it refers to more than just literary affairs.

TLOSTANOVA: How do you see the future of Russia, and does it have a future at all?

MAMEDOV: Prophesy is a thankless task and can be even dangerous at times. First, prophesies are seldom accurate and almost always need to be later edited by the contemporaries. Second, it is a certain kind of programming—you attune people to a particular development of events. And a person should be free from anyone's interference. People should see themselves in the future, realize their roles, and construct them according to their own principles and experience, and not those imposed by Kremlin ideologies. Russia probably does have a future, but it would hardly be similar to how a decent person imagines it. Human world lives according to Karmic laws and no one can change this. In other words, what goes around comes around. Everything returns to you. We are aware of what exactly we have planted since the USSR collapsed. I say "we" because it is a collective karma.

Russia is not a young country, even if many historians think so and impose their vision onto the society. They say that we still have time to correct ourselves, that we are still green and young. We are having fun. Russia is "having fun" with all the associated consequences.

Nikolay Berdyaev singled out five periods in Russian history: Kiev, Tatar, Moscow, Petersburg and Bolshevik. I believe that since 1991 we have lived in the sixth Russia. Evidently at some historical juncture we, our ancestors had worked out the fifth Russian karma, but not completely it seems because we never used this historical chance [to become a free and just society]. Today's époque of restoration and recoil is a proof. The sixth Russia had not even shaped itself properly yet when it already started to look back at the fifth period in its most unfortunate manifestations which are used as our templates today. Can we stop this process? I do not know. I only know that such processes are usually stopped at the cost of incredible sacrifices. Is it possible to avoid them? It probably is if the society and the power are both mature enough to induce and accept the changes . . . But instead we witness the opposite processes. In the best scenario it would bring a slow dying. And then the sixth Russia would turn out to be shorter than the fifth. How much shorter? It is better to pray for the country and for ourselves than tell fortunes.

Why are ye silent? Cry, Long live the tsar Dimítry Ivánovich!

(*The* People *are silent.*)

—Alexander Pushkin, *Boris Godunov*

CONCLUSION

People Are Silent . . .

I started this book with a rather pessimistic analysis of the futureless ontology reigning in the vast spaces of external imperial difference and its multiple colonial otherness. The futureless ontology leaves us with no hope indeed, unless we delink from one of modernity's favorite deceptions—that of the necessarily happy future—and decide to perform instead a radical return to the past that, to quote Zapatistas through Rolando Vázquez (2015), disrupts the hegemony of modernity. In Amerindian tempo-local models, the past is in front of us rather than behind us. It is not frozen and dead, closed and museumized. It is a living and breathing temporality that we know, in contrast with the unknown future, and this awareness is radically affecting our lives, offering a well of alternatives and giving us strength to live in the present and build our future. Therefore, it is crucial to reflect first on our uses of the troubled pasts if we intend to have any future. And this is what the former and present empires and their aftermaths are reluctant to allow.

Yet the local communities and individuals must do crucial work on memory, on historical traumas and restless ghosts that continue to consume us and erase our future. In the context of external imperial difference and its multiple colonial difference it means to engage in a painstaking labor of critical self-reflection and cultivation of courage to admit our responsibility for the past and the future. This radical delinking from the dogmas of neoliberal, socialist, nationalist, and other modern/colonial discourses would have to be grounded in the acceptance of the right to difference as the foundational principle of relational ontology and ethics and in the shift from the will to power that seems once again to be winning over the "will to life" (Dussel 2008, 78) in the contemporary world as a necessary requirement for bringing the present "defuturing" tendencies to a halt.

Decolonization of collective and personal memory is an extremely difficult task in which decolonial art, problematizing the official versions of history, can play a key role. It is a painful work asking for ruthless self-criticism. Paradoxically the colonized themselves often oppose this process. The surrogate of memory and the simulacrum of ethnic culture offered to the post-Soviet zombified nations, naturalize humiliation and cut off the ability to think critically.

Decolonizing memories and existence through art, entails a restoration of the artist's and the audience's agency—their right and ability to finally make their own choices and decide what to remember and how; to realize who we are and why were we brought into this world. Such decolonial creative acts inevitably address the spatial and corporeal memory and the memory of objects constantly traversing and problematizing the boundaries and leakages between human and nonhuman, animate and inanimate. The decolonial cathartic power of art then is realized through resisting and re-existing moves as forms of embodied memories, evoking the most primal affects—sonic, visual, olfactory, tactile, causing uncontrollable avalanches of previously censored remembrances that stubbornly reemerge.

Such decolonial work could potentially result in responsibility, independence, freedom, and maturity. And it should take place on different levels, including the level of intellectuals' carefully analyzing and reflecting on decolonial social movements rather than imposing ready-made solutions and tailored models on them. However, social movements and political society at large in contemporary post-Soviet states—both postcolonial and postimperial—are notoriously weak, demoralized, and marginalized, if they exist at all. Are there any remaining channels for decolonial potentialities in the space of the external imperial difference and its multiple colonial differences then? Once again, art seems to be one of the very few

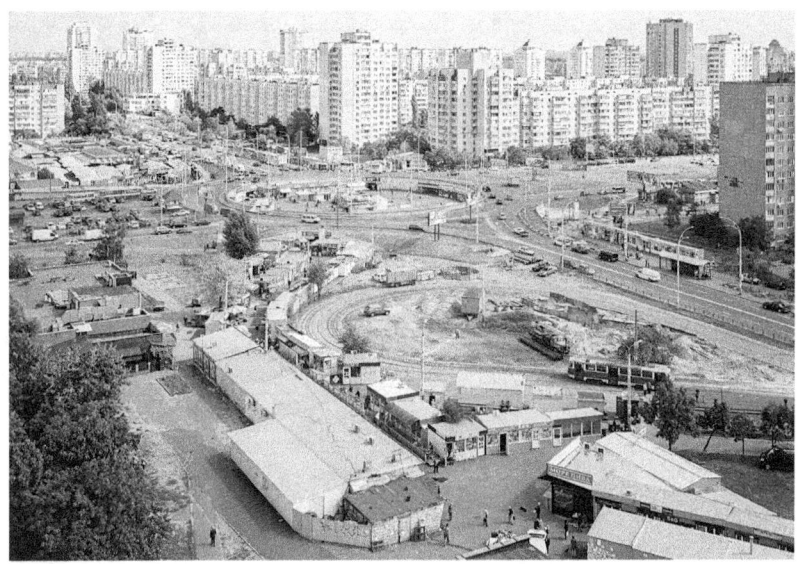

FIG. CONC.1 Egor Rogalev, *Situation No. 15.* Kiev, 2014. Archival photographic print in various editions; dimensions variable. From the photo series *Synchronicity.* Courtesy of the artist.

such channels. According to Caribbean writer Wilson Harris (1995, 378), in colonial spaces history is often buried in the art of imagination. It is only through allegories, symbols, and metaphors that we can tell an alternative narrative and not be killed or incarcerated. Yet, as discussed earlier, metaphorical expressions are also strangely more effective than bare facts because they call directly to our emotions and sensibilities thus launching a painful process of mental and existential liberation. And the first steps of this process are already visible in the works of many artists touched upon in this book.

Immanuel Kant (1996 [1684]) famously defined the Enlightenment as "man's emergence from his self-imposed nonage. Nonage is the inability to use one's own understanding without another's guidance. This nonage is self-imposed if its cause lies not in lack of understanding but in indecision and lack of courage to use one's own mind without another's guidance." Kant's definition is surprisingly fitting for the post-Soviet situation of voluntary self-colonization by various nationalist and imperial dogmas and myths keeping the population enchanted and therefore enslaved.

Reflecting on similar problems, but doing it from the underside of modernity, Frantz Fanon (1963, 316) doubted the ability of humanity to grow up and take responsibility for the world and for itself, yet he endorsed the necessity for the people of the global South to stop imitating Europe and catching up with it, and start "inventing and making discoveries" to "advance humanity a step further." Yet Fanon's call has largely remained a dream; as he analyzed the psychoses and neuroses of victims and torturers in the Algerian War of Independence, Fanon himself had to admit that it was hardly possible for them to become free of violence. "Their future is mortgaged," he wrote (Fanon 1963, 22).

Is this also true of the external imperial difference then? Are we forever marked by the apathy and inertia of the raped slave for whom the only escape could be into a "phenomenological disappearance" (Yampolsky 1999), placing one between death and enslavement, and ultimately making us invisible once again inside and outside the repressive system? One of the most talented and relentless critics of the Russian paradigm of violence, the late film director Aleksei German (2008), formulated this diagnosis even more harshly: "We are a raped, a prison-bitched country, and we forgave and forgot our humiliation and did not repent, did not ask for any retribution."

The main decolonial task for the former Soviet spaces, then, is precisely to overcome this persistent paradigm of violence, humiliation, and dispensability of human lives, and to find the courage to realize the extent of our bondage and start on the long and hard path away from fear and violence back to ourselves. This would mean learning not only to resist but also, most important, to re-exist. Russian human rights activist Yuri Kazakov (2004, 144) called this phenomenon a gene of violence—or one can say an apologia of violence—both from above and from the bottom, from the state and from the political opposition. This model is endlessly reproduced in different political forms, but its essence remains the same: the totality of violence cancels the question of ethics in political actions. In Kazakov's (2004, 144) words, "Post-Soviet Russia [and a number of other post-Soviet countries] has not become a country of mass repentance, the blame for its internal phlebotomy has been always shifted in the mass consciousness to some 'elites,' at best resolutely taking any personal responsibility off their shoulders. As a result, in public opinion we have an explosive mixture of social (civil) dystrophy and national and interethnic unrest, and finally, the all-penetrating sense of injustice." As long as this is true, de-imperialization, and hence decolonization, of thinking, being, and perception will never take place.

In the introduction, I touched on some of the reasons for the feebleness of the Russian protests of 2011–13 and the subsequent channeling of their energies by those in power. Indeed, small-scale social protests are doomed by definition because they avoid entering the political sphere. Likewise, the nonsystemic opposition has been consistently fragmented and unsuccessful in its exclusive focusing on politics and its refusal to deal with social and economic issues.[1] However, the shared protest against the fraudulent presidential election was not enough to make allies of the ultra-left and the ultra-right, of nationalist and neoliberal groups. It is symptomatic that none of the Russian "Occupies" has ever attempted to cooperate with each other or build coalitions afterwards.

In the closing months of 2016 when I was writing these words, almost three years after the strangling of the last protest wave, it has become clear that the wars in Ukraine and Syria could no longer help the Russian regime distract people's attention from growing economic instability and social unrest. Parliamentary elections in September 2016 demonstrated the actual crisis of legitimacy and the real attitude of citizens toward those in power. The majority of Russians simply ignored the election, which had record low turnouts. People do not believe elections can be used as a factor of change, and they refuse to be part of the election farce as well. The remaining low percentage of those who voted was comprised of completely dependent people—pensioners, students, prison inmates, soldiers, employees of state organizations—who did not have even a minimal choice.

Oppositional political scientist Andrey Piontkovsky wrote on September 21, 2016 at Kasparov.ru oppositional internet portal:

> Absence from the elections is a conscious form of expressing your attitude to power and its fake procedures. . . . It has become an international meme that Putin is supported by 86 percent of the population. . . . But what is support? It is a readiness to die for him at the barricades if someone attempts to displace him. Let us not require so much. There is a minimum degree of possible support—to show up at the election and vote for your leader's party. If one is not capable of doing this what kind of adherent of Putin is he then? Voting is an indirect but rather accurate opinion poll. . . . The turnout was 36 percent, and the United Russia got 40 percent. This means that Putin's real rating is 14 percent rather than 86 percent. (Piontkovsky 2016)

To me this change is an indication of another important phenomenon that is crucial for the emergence of decolonial drives in the space of external

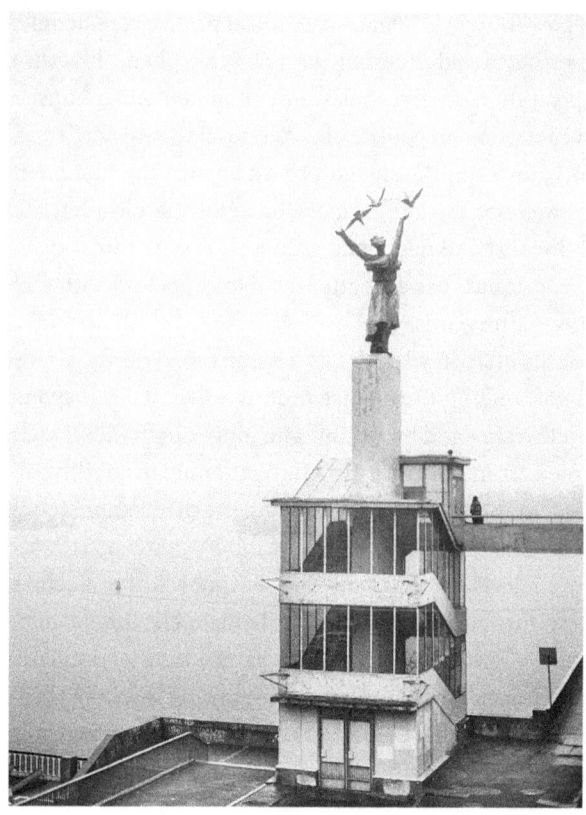

FIG. CONC.2 Egor Rogalev, *Situation No. 7.* Kiev, 2009. Archival photographic print in various editions; dimensions variable. From the photo series *Synchronicity.* Courtesy of the artist.

imperial difference. To put it simply, it is the phenomenon of silence as a political position, or even silence as a form of resistance and a promise of re-existence. South-African Nobel Prize laureate J.M. Coetzee in his postcolonial rereading of Daniel Defoe's famous novel fantasizes of Robinson Crusoe cutting off Friday's tongue for being arrogant and therefore dooming him forever to silence and inability to be born and become himself (Coetzee 1986). Yet it is also possible that Friday remains opaque of his own will and simply refuses to speak with Robinson. In the case of many post-Soviet/postcolonial groups, such a silence can be also a form of resistance and a first step in the direction of regaining their true sense of selfhood, their long-suffering human dignity that has always been a target of colonial and neocolonial rulers. The damage is not irreparable. For all of us who were, and sometimes still are, colonized by the Russian/Soviet/ post-Soviet empires, the path, again, will be long and complex, and we are at the start. Yet there is hope of re-existence.

Silence understood as a way of resistance reverberates with Alexander Pushkin's controversial, Shakespearian historical drama *Boris Godunov* (1918 [1825]), which famously ends with the death of Tsar Boris; the rise to power of the so-called False Dmitry; and the beginning of the period of unrest after which the Romanov dynasty came to power. The closing line of the play has been a subject of many conflicting interpretations, from an essentialist proof of Russians' slavish nature to seeing silence as a tangible realization of anger and an elementary form of confrontation. After all, the people who have just learned of the assassination of the previous ruler's family by the new tsar, and who are invited to praise the False Dmitry, respond to this call with terrified silence rather than obedience. The question is, How much fear and how much resistance does this silence contain?

In the present context of the post-Soviet silences I prefer to interpret this phenomenon as an intermediate position of neither-nor, of no more and not yet, from which a re-existence can still be born if some of the decolonial drives have a chance to evolve in the near future. Wendy Brown (1996, 197) refers to this intermediate state in an interesting way: "The historical-political place of silence for collective subjects emerging into history is this crossed one—a place of potentially pleasurable reprieve in newly acquired zones of freedom and privacy, yet a place of 'freedom from,' that is not yet freedom to make the world."

This disquieting yet promising note of silence is the first humble step toward future re-existence. This tendency once again is represented most graphically in post-Soviet art with the two examples from which I would like to wrap up this book. The first one represents the trajectory of the mainstream homogenizing actionist tradition, stemming from the space of the imperial difference and thus erasing many significant nuances. The second is an example of decolonial art, growing from the exteriority of colonial otherness and focusing on the nuances of difference and intersections of suppressions.

The first example is found in the works of the performance artist Pyotr Pavlensky, which are known and understood worldwide due to their posterlike actionist simplicity and straightforward message: the struggle with the regime's most recognizable features, such as censorship and shrinking freedom of speech and expression for artists, as well as other citizens. Such was his *Seam* (2012), in which Pavlensky stitched his own mouth shut with a coarse thread and stood for a long time in a picket line in front of Saint Petersburg's Kazan Cathedral to protest the incarceration of members of the feminist punk band Pussy Riot. In his famous *Fixation* (2013), the naked artist, in the best tradition of corporeal actionism, nailed his own scrotum to Red Square to protest the apathy and fatality of contemporary Russian society. Finally, in *Threat* (2015), Pavlensky, in an act of public arson, set fire to the doors of the Lubyanka building, headquarters of the KGB. This action resulted in a trial, and a disproportionately large fine was comically imposed on him for damaging the historically valuable building in which many prominent Russian cultural and societal figures were incarcerated or tortured. Pavlensky's art is no doubt radical and political. But it is also contained entirely within the realm of the immediate present and therefore is hardly decolonial. It falls instead into the paradigm of the futureless ontology (Walker 2014).

Aslan Gaisumov's decolonial works are less straightforward and simplified. They are multi-semantic and open to different interpretations and various temporalities, because they are not fixed in the actionist metaphysics of the presence, but try instead to reflect on the multiple pasts, without which there is no present or future. Gaisumov sees silence as an embryo of suppressed but survived resistance. He also focuses on the radical return in the form of placing the actual material archive of his denied past in a European museum as a dual gesture of setting himself free from the traumas of that past, yet at the same time, legitimating that past and making it impossible to deny.

These were the two main themes of the latest works shown at Gaisumov's personal exhibition at the Antwerp Museum of Contemporary Art in the summer of 2016 ("In Situ" 2016). The first work, the video installation *People of No Consequence*, is a reflection on the fate of the dying generation of Chechens who went through deportation in 1944, return in 1957, forceful amnesia and, several decades later, another series of Russian military campaigns that turned them into exiles and refugees once again in one short lifetime. Gaisumov gathered the elderly people whose lives went between these two exiles in an old Soviet house of culture that miraculously survived after many bombings and the subsequent construction boom of the present Chechen administration. The artist filmed these silent old people as they sat in the big hall and looked at its empty stage with fear, hope, anxiety, indifference, doom, and stubborn dignity in an attempt to capture the quintessence of their several decades of silence. The eyes, body movements, and postures of these people "of no consequence" betray their broken, intimidated, and humiliated condition. Yet they also reveal quiet happiness in being alive and back at home, even if only to die. Although they could not forget what was done to them, they were forbidden to remember or tell their stories. But I am not quick to condemn them for their reluctance to rebel. Having buried in the depths of collective unconsciousness the many "colonial wounds" (Anzaldúa 1999, 25), the unfinished repentances and revenges, the halfway decolonizations, they came to today's bitter humility and voluntary oblivion for lack of other choices. But their silence (or rather, a tacit consent not to discuss certain historical events) is not necessarily just a sign of colonized minds and bodies. Rather, it is a form of psychological self-defense or repression vacillating between amnesia and rejection. But it is not a final chord and not a requiem as long as there are artists like Gaisumov and wider, people of his generation who are willing to discuss these silences and relentlessly remind us of them in spite of all the efforts of official narratives to erase these lives of no consequence from history.

Gaisumov's second work, *Household*, consists of a big crate full of everyday objects, clothes, utensils, articles necessary for survival—in short all the real material things that the artist's family actually used during their long refugee life. It is a materialized past carefully packed and sent to the museum. The symbolism of this work is historically relational as it is an act of not even writing but sending back to the center. The deported Chechens who were dehumanized to the point of being completely objectified were sent to Central Asia in cargo and cattle cars. Gaisumov's reciprocal gesture of sending the meager objects of his family's homeless existence to a museum to finally get rid of embodied memories by making this past public and objectified and to prevent any further disembodiment and erasing of its palpable materiality is a decolonial radical return that functions on several levels at once. The artist who used to be in the position of a live object himself, remembers a similar destiny of his ancestors and commemorates this negative lineage capable of triggering emancipating drives and sensibilities through the parcel containing the embodied past. At the museum for permanent storage, the crates serve as a marker of the end of his refugee existence and an attempt to deposit the processed past that he wants to let go but not erase.

In this complex, multilayered, contradictory, and dynamic gesture that, unlike Pavlensky's works, is not confined to the metaphysics of the present but always communicates with the multiple living pasts, there is still hope for the creation of an alternative reality, a faith in re-existence. It is a forever open ending that refuses to dot the "i"s and therefore leaves us at least some options. Its radical return, together with the forever unfinished nature of constant becoming, makes Gaisumov's works truly decolonial. Even in the darkest moment, one of which we are experiencing now, freedom and dignity still prevail—at least, in the realm of decolonial transcendence of modernity/coloniality through the medium of art. This is already enough to cherish a hope.

A merciless purging of the grand imperial myths, with their inhumane, unsightly colonial lining, and a decolonizing of collective and personal memory are the only remaining paths to any positive future that will not be stuck with imperial difference. It is hard to imagine this future today from the midst of the darkest imperial moment of its imminent death and its stubborn clinging to life. Yet I do hope that even the phantom pains of the amputated empire will recede sooner than we imagine and a completely different geopolitics and corpo-politics of knowledge, being, and perception would (re)emerge. Multiple dependencies and intersections of oppression require a complex purification, in which the affective mechanisms are no less but more important than rational arguments. And the decolonial art, on which I mainly concentrated in this book acts as one of the most powerful agents of decoloniality and provides promising ways to prepare for and build the future.

NOTES

INTRODUCTION

1. The term "colonial difference" refers to the complex differential between empires and their colonies. Colonial difference is studied much more thoroughly than imperial difference in postcolonial theory and decolonial thought. Although the empire-colony dichotomy has been criticized time and again for its black-and-white simplicity, and a number of thinkers have attempted to complicate and problematize this binary in more dynamic reciprocal forms (see, e.g., Bhabha 1994; Ortiz 1995), the colonial difference in general has remained the most obvious, visual, and immediate representation of the power dynamics of modernity/coloniality.

Imperial difference disrupts the presumable homogeneity of imperial spatiality and complicates it by drawing attention to various complete or partial losers that, for various reasons, failed to fulfill their imperial missions in the post-Enlightenment modernity. As a result, they occupied second- or even third-class places within the modern imperial hierarchy and increasingly competed among themselves rather than with the winners. Occasional attempts to move up from the second division to the first, an interesting example of which was the USSR, invariably have been prevented and punished by the first-class imperial powers. Even if they retained economic and political independence, the losing empires were colonized intellectually, culturally, and existentially, often via efficient self-colonizing tools.

Similarly to colonial difference, which is sustained through the paradox of an essentially unattainable ideal of progress and an ultimate merging with imperial sameness, the sphere of imperial difference has repeatedly slid into an endless logic of catching up. Second-class empires have developed collective inferiority complexes and unhealthy compensating mechanisms, as well as besieged-camp ideologies and victory-in-defeat myths. Not incidentally, the liminal empires marked by imperial difference were located in Eurasia, which contains the most complex cultural, ethnic, religious, and economic intersections and nodal points. Usually these empires lacked important features of the successful modern imperial profile, such as Western Christianity, increasingly in its Protestant forms; capitalism, increasingly in its industrial, not mercantile, varieties; racial hierarchies that easily distinguished between subjects and so-called others; and last, but not least, the alphabetical and linguistic affinity, which seriously affected symbolic belonging to the ruling club.

2. I coined the term "Janus-faced empire" in the early 2000s in an attempt to explain the neurotic Russian imperial configuration as a polity that has never been allowed into the Western club but secretly, or openly, wants to be accepted. Today, the "Tatar dressed as a Frenchman," as the Russian imperial historian Vasily Klyuchevsky (2009) has described this identity, is lapsing into yet another chauvinistic cycle by bragging about its exaggerated "Asiatic" qualities. The devious and unreliable imperial Russian Janus has also been manipulative and strangely adaptable to different conditions, successfully imitating and appropriating other imperial models to balance its difficult divided positionality.

An imperial paradox, this Janus has been rich yet poor, providential yet failed, and always struggling and never quite succeeding in appropriating certain elements of modernity/coloniality. To survive, it has had to wear different masks for different partners—European and non-European. In a way, in the presence of Western Europe it has always felt like a colony and compensated for this by projecting an image of the Russian/Soviet colonizer as a champion of civilization, modernization, and, later, specifically socialist modernity into its own non-European colonies. Moreover, a complex internal hierarchy of intercolonial differences generated a variety of masks the empire wore to address each of the colonies. When Russia/the USSR was looking in the direction of its European frontiers (Finland, Poland, the Baltic littoral), it acted like an unconfident colonizer that was unable to practice imperial superiority or carry out civilizing missions because of its own lower position in the hierarchy of modernity. Looking to the East and to the South—the only remaining directions for its imperial expansion in the post-Enlightenment modern era, Russia/the USSR wore a different mask: that of a distorted "white man's burden," which Fyodor Dostoyevsky (1977, 35) described when he wrote, "In Europe we were hangers-on and slaves, whereas in Asia we shall go as masters." A special case of the complex interplay of the external imperial and colonial differences in the Janus-faced empire was represented in Russia's relations with the intermediary cases of Ukraine and Belarus, whose difference was deliberately erased and silenced to enhance the insecure Russian sameness. The inconfident Russian imperial identity asserted itself by denying the existence and forcefully assimilating these East Slavic ethnic cultures.

3. Arguments about whether it would be better to be colonized by Great Britain or by Russia and self-defensive statements about how lucky we are that we do not live in Afghanistan are typical illustrations of this sensibility in Central Asia.

4. "Make food for powder" is an idiom used by William Shakespeare in *Henry IV*. Falstaff says: "good enough to toss; food for powder, food for powder; they'll fill a pit as well as better." It is normally used to describe combatants who are cynically treated as unimportant lives who are easily sacrificed on the battlefield.

5. La Leyenda Negra (The Black Legend) was originally a biased representation of Spain in the historiography of its more successful European imperial rivals (Greer, Quilligan, Mignolo 2008). Here it is used to denote a general style of argumentation meant to demonize the adversary to construct a positive self-representation, habitually used in geopolitical rivalry.

6. Immigration has reached unprecedented numbers in Russia in the past several years and continues to grow. The latest wave has been more politically than economically induced—or, at least, the two factors play equal roles. In a sense, the regime is using the still open borders as a safety valve, to let off the steam. If dissidents, who also tend to be highly educated professionals, are able to leave and are doing so, the threat of revolution is considerably reduced.

7. In the months that passed between writing the first draft and the final version of this book, many more social and economic protests were taking place in the Russian provinces (but not so much in Moscow and Saint Petersburg, with an important exception of the schoolchildrens' and students' dominated revolts in the spring of 2017). Among them was the Krasnodar farmers' march on the Kremlin in the late summer of 2016, which was stopped abruptly and violently persecuted at a great distance from Moscow. The farmers, driving tractors, were protesting unlawful seizures of land and harvests by large businesses supported by corrupt local bureaucrats and police, which were leaving thousands of people bankrupt. Another example is the strike by truck drivers that was renewed on a massive scale in the spring of 2017 against the Platon electronic toll system, which assesses fees based on the weight of a truck's cargo and could lead to economic ruin for many truckers who own and operate their vehicles as independent contractors.

In these and other protests, the protesters have wanted to take their social and economic claims directly to the president; they believe that he is not aware of the iniquity that is being created and that, once he finds out, he will restore justice. Thus, rather than Russian government, the protesters target local officials or the West as their enemy. This reflects the stale Russian foundational political myth of the good tsar and the bad boyars that played such an important part in Stalinist times. Paradoxically, these protests are pro-Putin.

CHAPTER 1. The Decolonial Sublime

1. Rancière titled one of his latest books *Aisthesis: Scenes from the Aesthetic Regime of Art* (2013). However, in many ways it reiterates his original take on aesthetics.

2. Similarly to other concepts, creolization, which was originally coined outside the West and linked with particular local histories, was fruitfully theorized in the Caribbean tradition and later appropriated by Western theory as a fashionable term. It was subsequently used in mainstream texts mostly in its positive and quite superfluous interpretations, celebrating the fusion of cultural forms and their egalitarian interaction. In this case, persistent power hierarchies in the production of cultural patterns and the absorption and deformation of dependent cultures by dominant cultures, are virtually ignored. Paradoxically, in celebrating creolization Bourriaud appropriates and distorts it, erasing its asymmetries, painful struggles, and element of resistance.

Instead, he sees a smooth and continuous blending of everything and everyone in some anti-hierarchical altermodern space, which exists only in his own head. As a result, "creolization" turns into a floating or empty signifier, a sign behind which nothing lies.

I prefer a different understanding of "creolization," which is represented, among other sources, in *The Creolization of Theory*, edited by Françoise Lionnet and Shu-mei Shih: "The strength of the concept arises directly from its historical specificity. As a process that registers the history of slavery, plantation culture, colonization, settlement, forced migration, and most recently, the uneven global circulation of labor, creolization describes the encounter among peoples in a highly stratified terrain. So it is not just any transculturation but 'forced transculturation'" (Lionnet and Shih 2011, 25).

3. Here transmodernity is understood in Enrique Dussel's sense. He juxtaposes it to postmodernity and sees it as an alternative yet utopian space of thinking and acting (Dussel 2002). We could widen this juxtaposition to include Bourriaud's altermodernity, as well. Transmodernity overcomes modernity from the position of exteriority or border thinking instead of continuing its endless internal critique, which never problematizes the Eurocentric universalist progressivist totality of modernity as such. In the mechanism of the decolonial sublime, it is especially important that, in the process of delinking and subsequent re-existence, modernity be ultimately overcome.

CHAPTER 2. Post-Soviet Art

1. After 2010, the National Bolsheviks formed the core of a wider opposition political alliance known as The Other Russia.

2. Although Dugin was originally a member of Eduard Limonov's National Bolshevik Party, their paths soon diverged. Today Dugin represents the farthest-right, most statist, most fundamentalist discourse; although it has very little to do with the original concept of Eurasianism, it borrows the name and accentuates the nationalist and imperial sides of the sanctified geopolitics. Dugin is notoriously ridiculed for his advancement of the aggressive revanchist dream of the planetary geopolitical revenge presided by Russia, after which the lost and "hidden meta-continents will emerge from the depths of the past" and "geopolitics will become a sacred geography" (Dugin 1996, 36). In contrast with Limonov, who has been banned and persecuted, Dugin stands very close to the present Russian administration, often acting as a mouthpiece for populist imperial rhetoric.

3. Bombily blog, http://halfaman.livejournal.com/.

4. E-mail to the author, January 31, 2016.

5. Guslitsa is a former textile factory not far from Moscow that was built by a local businessman named Petrashov in 1908. It was abandoned and damaged in the post-Soviet years but in 2012 was bought by a family of businessmen who turned it into an art, cultural, and exhibition center; artists' residence; and home for several social movements and local community initiatives. In 2016, however, the artists, social activists, entrepreneurs, and owners of Guslitsa were forced out by so-called raiders, who attempted to turn the facility into a warehouse. Luckily the artists were eventually able to defend their creation.

6. E-mail to the author, January 31, 2016.

7. E-mail to the author, January 31, 2016.

8. E-mail to the author, January 31, 2016.

9. The Uzbek director Nazim Abbasov's film *Eternity* (2005), which focuses on the potters' craft and lifestyle, provides interesting, poetic documentation of such a surviving indigenous cosmological tradition as expressed through art.

10. See Laura Bulian Gallery, http://www.laurabuliangallery.com/index.html.

11. E-mail to the author, November 5, 2010.

12. E-mail to the author, November 5, 2010.

CHAPTER 4. Vyacheslav Akhunov

1. Alexander Volkov (1886–1957) was a Russian avant-garde artist who spent his life in Uzbekistan and merged typically Central Asian topics and subjects, which he often interpreted in Gauguinian Orientalist ways, with suprematist and cubist-futuristic aesthetics.

2. From *chapan*, a traditional Uzbek men's robe. The chapan is a standard souvenir given to important guests in Uzbekistan as a sign of respect.

3. The exhibition took place in Saint Petersburg in February 2016 at the private gallery Lyuda. It was titled, "You Will Be Living Under . . . ."

4. Akhunov refers here to the unique State Art Museum of the Republic of Karakalpakstan, named after I. V. Savitsky, which holds the second-largest collection of Russian avant-garde in the world.

5. Mukhamad Salikh (Salih) is one of the Uzbek political opposition leaders and a poet who has political asylum in Norway and lives in Turkey. Repeated attempts have been made to assassinate, arrest, and extradite him.

CHAPTER 5. Afanassy Mamedov

1. Maxim Gorky Literature Institute in Moscow.

2. The novel is *Cinnabar* (*kinovar* in Russian, which links phonetically with *kino*, or cinema) and was published in 2015 in the journal *Druzhba Narodov*.

CONCLUSION

Epigraph: Pushkin 1918 (1825), 117.

1. In the protest wave of 2011–13 this fragmentation resulted in a multiplication of "Occupy" groups. They chose their own urban spaces with which to be identified. The best-known example was Occupy Abai, which hijacked the Kazakh poet's name and monument in central Moscow to stand for the struggle for human dignity and the right to choose one's destiny.

REFERENCES

Abbasov, Nazym. 2005. *Eternity*. Film. Gala-Film Studio and National Agency Uzbek Cinema, Tashkent, Uzbekistan.

Albán Achinte, Adolfo. 2006. *Texiendo textos y saberes. Cinco hijos para pensar los estudios culturales, la colonialidad y la interculturalidad*. Popayán, Colombia: Editorial Universidad del Cauca, Colección Estiodios (Inter)culturales.

———. 2009. "Artistas indígenas y afrocolombianos: Entre las memorias y las cosmo-visiones. Estéticas de la re-existencia." In *Arte y estética en la encrucijada descolonial*, ed. Zulma Palermo, 83–112. Buenos Aires: Del Siglo.

Alexievich, Svetlana. 2013. *Vremya Second Hand* [Secondhand Time]. Moscow: Vremya.

Ames, Mark. 2011. "The Massacre Everyone Ignored." *The Exiled*, December 19. Accessed September 15, 2017. http://exiledonline.com/the-massacre-everyone-ignored-70-striking-oil-workers-killed-in-kazakhstan-by-us-supported-dictator/.

Anderson, Benedict. 1983. *Imagined Communities: Reflections on the Origin and Spread of Nationalism*. London: Verso.

Anzaldúa, Gloria. 1999. *Borderlands/La Frontera: The New Mestiza*. San Francisco: Aunt Lute.

Baumgarten, Alexander Gottlieb. 1750. *Aesthetica*. Frankfurt: Impensis. I. C. Kleyb. Accessed December 15, 2016. https://archive.org/details/aestheticascripoobaumgoog.

Bhabha, Homi. 1994. *The Location of Culture*. London: Routledge.

Bourriaud, Nicolas. 2002a. *Postproduction: Culture as Screenplay: How Art Reprograms the World*. New York: Lukas and Sternberg.

———. 2002b. *Relational Aesthetics*. Dijon, France: Les Presses du Reel.

———. 2009. *Altermodern Manifesto*. Tate triennial. Accessed December 15, 2016. http://www.tate.org.uk/britain/exhibitions/altermodern/manifesto.shtm.

Brooks, David. 2000. *Bobos in Paradise: The New Upper Class and How They Got There*. New York: Simon and Schuster.

Brown, Wendy. 1996. "In the 'Folds of Our Own Discourse': The Pleasures and Freedoms of Silence." *University of Chicago Law School Roundtable* 3, Iss.1. Article 8: 185–97.

Butler, Judith. 1997. *Excitable Speech: A Politics of the Performative*. London: Routledge.

Coetzee, John M. 1986. *Foe*. New York: Viking.

Curtis, Neil G.W. 2012. "Universal Museums, Museum Objects and Repatriation: The Tangled Stories of Things." In *Museum Studies: An Anthology of Contexts*, 2nd ed., ed. Bettina Messias Carbonell, 73–81. London: Wiley Blackwell.

Deleuze, Gilles, and Félix Guattari. 1993. *A Thousand Plateaus: Capitalism and Schizophrenia*. Minneapolis: University of Minnesota Press.

Dilthey, Wilhelm. 1991. "Introduction to the Human Sciences." In *Selected Works*, vol. 1, eds. Rudolf A. Makkreel and Frithjof Rodi. Princeton, NJ: Princeton University Press.

Dostoyevsky, Fyodor. 1977 [1881]. "Geok-Tepe. Chto takoye dlya nas Azia?" [Geok-Tepe. What is Asia for Us?] "Dnevnik Pisatelja" [Writer's Diary]. *Complete Works, Volume 27*, 32–35. Leningrad: Nauka.

Du Bois, W. E. B. 1903. *The Souls of Black Folk*. Chicago: A. C. McClurg.

Dugin, Alexander. 1996. *Misterii Yevrazii* [Mysteries of Eurasia]. Moscow: Arktogeya.

Dussel, Enrique. 1985. *Philosophy of Liberation*, trans. Aquilina Martinez and Christine Morkovsky. Eugene, OR: Wipf and Stock.

———. 1996. *The Underside of Modernity: Apel, Ricoeur, Rorty, Taylor, and the Philosophy of Liberation*. New York: Humanity.

———. 2002. "World-System and 'Trans'-Modernity." *Nepantla: Views from South* 3, no. 2:221–44.

———. 2008. *Twenty Theses on Politics*. Durham, NC: Duke University Press.

Epshtein, Alec D. 2012. *Totalnaya "Voina." Art-aktivism Epokhi Tandemokratii* [Total War. Art-Activism of the Tandemocracy Époque]. Moscow: Umlaut Network.

Etkind, Alexander. 2011. *Internal Colonization: Russia's Imperial Experience*. London: Polity.

Fanon, Frantz. 1963. *The Wretched of the Earth*, trans. Constance Farrington. New York: Grove Weidenfeld.

———. 1967. *Black Skin. White Masks*, trans. Charles Lamm Markmann. New York: Grove.

Fomenko, Andrei. 2013. "O Gorakh i Geroiakh. Beseda s Erbossynom Mel'dibekovym i Dastanom Kozhakhmetovym" [On Mountains and Heroes: A Conversation with Yerbossyn Meldibekov and Dastan Kozhakhmetov]. *Art 1. Visual Daily*, October 16. Accessed December 15, 2016. http://art1.ru/art/o-gorax-i-geroyax.

Fry, Tony. 2011. *Design as Politics*. Oxford, New York: Berg.

Gamzatova, Patimat R. 2009. "Aktualniye Problemy Iskusstva v Musulmanskom Areale Stran SNG v Nachale 21 Veka" [Topical Problems of Art in the Muslim Area of CIS Countries in the Early Twenty-First Century]. In *Iskusstvo Turkskogo Mira. Istoki i Evolutsija Khudozhestvennoi Kulturi Turkskikh Narodov* [The Art of the Turkic World: Sources and Evolution of the Artistic Culture of the Turkic People], ed. Patimat Sultanova, 56–67. Kazan, Russian Federation: Zaman.

German, Aleksei. 2008. "Germanologia." Interview for the project *An Other Cinema.* Accessed December 16, 2016. https://yandex.ru/video/search?text=германология.

Gogol, Nikolai. 1835 [2009]. *Viy.* Kharkov, Ukraine: Mikko.

Gordon, Lewis R. 2000. "Existential Borders of Anonymity and Superfluous Invisibility." In *Existentia Africana*, 153–63. New York: Routledge.

———. 2007. "Problematic People and Epistemic Decolonization: Toward the Postcolonial in Africana Political Thought." In *Postcolonialism and Political Theory*, ed. Nalini Persram, 121–42. New York: Lexington.

Greer, Margaret R., Maureen Quilligan, Walter D. Mignolo, eds. 2008. *Rereading the Black Legend: The Discourses of Religious and Racial Difference in the Renaissance Empires.* Chicago: University of Chicago Press.

Groys, Boris. 2008. "Beyond Diversity: Cultural Studies and Its Post-Communist Other." In Boris Groys, *Art Power*, 149–63. Cambridge, MA: MIT Press.

Hardt, Michael, and Antonio Negri. 2005. *Multitude: War and Democracy in the Age of Empire.* New York: Penguin.

Harris, Wilson. 1995. "The Limbo Gateway." In *The Post-Colonial Studies Reader*, ed. Bill Ashcroft, Gareth Griffiths, and Helen Tiffin, 378–82. London: Routledge.

Holquist, Michael. 1994. "Corrupt Originals: The Paradox of Censorship." *PMLA* 109, no. 1:14–25.

"In Situ: Aslan Gaisumov—People of No Consequence." 2016. Exhibition curated by Anders Kreuger, May 20–September 4, Antwerp Museum of Contemporary Art. Accessed December 16, 2016. https://www.muhka.be/programme/detail/550-in-situ-aslan-gaisumov-people-of-no-consequence.

Jirgens, Karl. 2006. "Fusions of Discourse: Postcolonial/Postmodern Horizons in Baltic Culture." In *Baltic Postcolonialism*, ed. Violeta Kelertas, 45–82. Amsterdam: Rodopi.

Kalnačs, Benedikts. 2016a. "Comparing Colonial Differences: Baltic Literary Cultures as Agencies of Europe's Internal Others." *Journal of Baltic Studies* 47, no. 1:15–30.

———. 2016b. *20th Century Baltic Drama: Postcolonial Narratives, Decolonial Options.* Bielefeld: Aisthesis.

Kant, Immanuel. 1951 (1790). *The Critique of Judgment.* New York: Hafner.

———. 1996 (1784). "An Answer to the Question: What Is Enlightenment?" In *Practical Philosophy*, tran. Mary J. Gregor, 11–22. Cambridge: Cambridge University Press.

Kazakov, Yuri. 2004. "Obraz Smerti kak Stil Zhizni" [The Image of Death as a Lifestyle]. In *Sotsialnoye Nasiliye i Tolerantnost: Realnost i Media-obrazy* [Social Violence and Tolerance: Reality and Media Images], ed. Joseph Dzyaloshinsky, 140–47. Moscow: IIC.

Klyuchevsky, Vasily. 2009. *Kurs Russkoy Istorii* [A Course in Russian History]. Moscow: Alfa-Kniga.

Kołodziejczyk, Dorota, and Cristina Sandru. 2012. "Introduction: On Colonialism, Communism and East-Central Europe—Some Reflections." *Journal of Postcolonial Writing* 48, no. 2:113–16.

Kovačević, Nataša. 2008. *Narrating Post/Communism: Colonial Discourse and Europe's Borderline Civilization.* London: Routledge.

Lazarus, Neil. 2012. "Spectres Haunting: Postcommunism and Postcolonialism." *Journal of Postcolonial Writing* 48, no. 2:117–29.

Levine, Michael. 1995. *Writing through Repression*. Baltimore: Johns Hopkins University Press.

Lionnet, Françoise. 2012. "The Mirror and the Tomb. Africa, Museums, and Memory." In *Museum Studies: An Anthology of Contexts*, 2nd ed., ed. Bettina Messias Carbonell, 189–99. London: Wiley Blackwell.

Lionnet, Françoise, and Shu-mei Shih, eds. 2011. *The Creolization of Theory*. Durham, NC: Duke University Press.

Lotman, Yuri. 2002. *Istoriya i Tipologiya Russkoi Kulturi* [History and Typology of Russian Culture]. Saint Petersburg: Iskusstvo SPB.

Maffesoli, Michel. 1988. *Le Temps des Tribus*. Paris: Méridiens Klincksieck.

Makhacheva, Taus. 2011. "Art Persona." *Art Chronicle*, December 9. Interview by Valery Ledenev. Accessed December 16, 2016. http://artchronika.ru/persona/таус -махачева-«я-могу-попасть-в-те-сфер.

———. 2015. "A Longing for a Superhero." Where Is the Line between Us? Third International Conference of the Garage Museum of Contemporary Art, March 21. Accessed December 16, 2016. https://www.youtube.com/watch?v=cKFmKgcspoc.

Matveyev, Ilya. 2016. "Russia, Inc." *ODR: Russia and Beyond*, March 16. Accessed September 17, 2017. https://www.opendemocracy.net/od-russia/ilya-matveev /russia-inc.

Mignolo, Walter D. 2000. "Coloniality at Large: Time and the Colonial Difference." In *Time in the Making and Possible Futures*, ed. Enrique Rodríguez Larreta, 237–72. Rio de Janeiro: Unesco-International Social Science Council-Educam.

———. 2011. "Geopolitics of Sensing and Knowing: On (De)Coloniality, Border Thinking, and Epistemic Disobedience." European Institute for Progressive Cultural Policies website, September. Accessed December 16, 2016. http://eipcp.net/transversal /0112/mignolo/en.

Mignolo, Walter D., and Arturo Escobar, eds. 2009. *Globalization and the Decolonial Option*. London: Routledge.

Mignolo, Walter, and Pablo Gómez, eds. 2012. *Estéticas y opción decolonial*. Bogotá: Editorial UD.

Moraga, Cherríe, and Gloria Anzaldúa, eds. 1981. *This Bridge Called My Back: Writings by Radical Women of Color*. San Francisco: Aunt Lute.

Mureşan, Ciprian. 2004. *Leap into the Void, after Three Seconds*. Photography, gelatin silver print on paper. Tate Gallery.

Nikolayev, Anton. 2011. "The Chronicles of Virtual Revolt. Artivism and Actionism," June 6. Accessed December 16, 2016. http://halfaman.livejournal.com/510998 .html.

Ortiz, Fernando. 1995. *Cuban Counterpoint: Tobacco and Sugar*. Durham, NC: Duke University Press.

Parshikov, Andrei. 2008. "Moskovsky Infantilism" [Moscow Infantilism]. *Art Strelka*, July 8. Accessed December 16, 2016. http://www.artstrelka.ru/galleries.page ?exhibitionID=426&menu=3&id=6.

Piontkovsky, Andrey. 2016. Interview posted on the website Kasparov.ru, September 21. Accessed December 17, 2016. http://www.kasparov.ru/material.php?id =57E177352F976&section_id=4B693228DBEC.

Pucherová, Dobrota, and Róbert Gáfric, eds. 2015. *Postcolonial Europe? Essays on Post-Communist Literatures and Cultures.* Leiden: Brill Rodopi.

Pushkin, Alexander. 1960. "Kapitanskaja Dochka" [Captain's Daughter]. In *Complete Works in Ten Volumes*, vol. 5, 286–411. Moscow: State Publishing House of Creative Writings.

———. 1918 [1825]. *Boris Godunov: A Drama in Verse*, trans. Alfred Hayes. London: Kegan Paul, Trench, Trubner.

Rancière, Jacques. 2009. "Contemporary Art and the Politics of Aesthetics." In *Communities of Sense: Rethinking Aesthetics and Politics*, eds. Beth Hinderliter, Vered Maimon, Jaleh Mansoor, and Seth McCormick, 31–50. Durham, NC: Duke University Press.

———. 2013. *Aisthesis: Scenes from the Aesthetic Regime of Art.* London: Verso.

Robbins, Bruce. 2002. "The Sweatshop Sublime." PMLA 117, no. 1:84–97.

Shchapov, Afanasy. 1906. *Sochineniya* [Writings]. Saint Petersburg: M. V. Pirozhkov.

Shimov, Yaroslav. 2016. "Slavic Lecture and Other Lies." *Radio Freedom*, January 26.

Slapšak, Svetlana. 2012. "Women, Yugoslavia, Anticommunist Narcosis and New Colonialism: Maps, Roads, Exits." In *Feminist Critical Interventions: Thinking Heritage, Decolonizing, Crossings*, ed. Biljana Kašić, Jelena Petrović, Sandra Prlenda, and Svetlana Slapšak, 40–49. Zagreb, Croatia: Red Athena University Press.

Solovyev, Vladimir. 2002. "Russkaja Ideya." In Yevgeny Vasilyev, ed., *Russkaja Ideya* [The Russian Idea], 227–56. Moscow: Iris.

Spalding, Julian. 2002. *The Poetic Museum: Reviewing Historic Collections.* Munich: Prestel.

Tlostanova, Madina. 2003. *A Janus-Faced Empire.* Moscow: Blok.

———. 2007. "Imperial-Colonial Chronotope: Istanbul-Baku-Khurramabad." *Cultural Studies* 21, nos. 2–3:406–27.

———. 2014. "Why the Post-Socialist Cannot Speak: On Caucasian Blacks, Imperial Difference and Decolonial Horizons." In *Postcoloniality-Decoloniality-Black Critique: Joints and Fissures*, ed. Sabine Broeck and Carsten Junker, 159–73. Frankfurt: Campus.

———. 2015. "Can the Post-Soviet Think? On Coloniality of Knowledge, External Imperial and Double Colonial Difference." *Intersections* 1, no. 2:38–58.

Tlostanova, Madina, and Walter Mignolo. 2009. "On Pluritopic Hermeneutics, Trans-Modern Thinking, and Decolonial Philosophy." *Encounters* 1, no. 1:11–27.

———. 2012. *Learning to Unlearn: Decolonial Reflection from Eurasia and the Americas.* Columbus: Ohio State University Press.

Vázquez, Rolando. 2015. "Decolonial Aesthesis Overcoming the Post/Human." In *The Human Condition: International Interdisciplinary Project*, National Center for Contemporary Art, Moscow, November 27. Accessed December 17, 2016. https://www .youtube.com/watch?v=RKEzFaunzog.

Vishmidt, Marina, Tiago Bom, Vanessa Ohlraun, Ayatgali Tuleubek, Susanne Winterling, eds. 2013. *Winter: Poetics and Politics.* Oslo: Mousse Publishing.

Walker, Shaun. 2014. "Petr Pavlensky: Why I Nailed My Scrotum to Red Square." *The Guardian*, February 5.

Wilson, Frederic. 1993. Statement for the Whitney Museum of American Art's Biennial, New York, qtd. in James Putnam, *Art and Artifact: The Museum as Medium*, 101. London: Thames and Hudson, 2001.

Yampolsky, Mikhail. 1999. "Iszheznoveniye Kak Forma Suschestvovaniya" [Disappearance as a Form of Existence]. *Kinovedcheskiye Zapiski* [Notes in Cinema Studies] no. 44:21–27. Accessed November 25, 2016. http://kinozapiski.ru.jumper.mtw.ru/ru/article/sendvalues/656.

INDEX

Abbasov, Nazym, 133n9

ABC (The Alphabet of Totalitarianism) (Akhunov painting), 95

Absheron Chronicles (Mamedov), 110

activism, 7, 21, 22–24, 35, 37–38, 39, 69, 75, 87, 97. *See also* artivism; specific individuals

aesthesis: decolonial, 22–24, 28–31, 35, 36–37, 49–64; use of term, 25, 26–27

aesthetics, 25–29, 31, 39, 45, 85, 88

Ainso, Sirje, 73

Akhunov, Vyacheslav, 23, 42–44, 84–104, *89*, *95*, *102*

Albán Achinte, Adolfo, 29–30

Alexievich, Svetlana, 9

altermodernity, 27–28, 29

ancestral homes, 115

Anderson, Benedict, 18

anti-Americanism, 12

Anzaldúa, Gloria, 29

Apotheosis of War, The (Vereshchagin painting), 43

Armenian Queering Yerevan Collective, 75

art: activism through, 7, 22–24, 37–38, 39, 69, 87, 97; on decolonial/de-Sovietizing impulses, 6; as decolonial force, 22–24, 39–42; ethnic, 31, 39, 42; official vs. nonofficial, 86; postethnic, 42; resistance through, 41–42, 70–71, 80, 83, 120. *See also* aesthesis; aesthetics

artivism, use of term, 22, 37–38

Atabekov, Said, 44–45

Atget, Eugène, 67

Azerbaijan, 49–50, 105

Badalov, Babi, 50

Baltic countries, 5, 130n2. *See also* specific countries

Baumgarten, Alexander, 25

Bazargaliev, Kuanysh, 47

Belarus, 130n2

belonging, 7, 33, 78–79, 130n1

Benjamin, Walter, 67, 81

Berdyaev, Nikolay, 117

Bhabha, Homi, 66

Bird Gamayun, The (Vasnetsov painting), 55–56

Black Legend, 14–18

Blind Alley (Akhunov video), 43

Blok, Alexander, 106

Bobos in Paradise (Brooks), 27

Bombily Art Group, 34, 35–39

Boris Godunov (Pushkin), 119, 125

Borubayeva, Burbukan, 103

Bourriaud, Nicolas, 27–28, 131–32nn2–3

Brecht, Bertolt, 82

Brooks, David, 27

Brown, Wendy, 125

Buddhism, 112

Bulgaria, 13, 15

Burchuladze, Zaza, 14
Butler, Judith, 23

Carceri, Le (Siib series), 81
Carpet (Makhacheva video), 51
Caspian Sea (Makhacheva artwork), 52–53, 54
Caucasus, post-socialist, 5–6, 34, 42, 49–64
Cellophane Painting (Suleimenova series), 48
censorship, 23, 38, 87, 98, 103, 125
Central Asia, post-socialist, 5–6, 34, 42–49, 93.
    See also specific countries
Certeau, Michel de, 67
Chaim, L' (journal), 105
chauvinism, 34, 130n2
Chechnya, 61–64, 126–27
Coetzee, John M., 124
collective identity, 19, 26–27, 29, 93
colonial difference: imperial difference
    and, 3–4, 10, 11–12, 39–42, 65–66, 120,
    129–30n1; use of term, 129n1
colonial wounds, 127
coloniality: ethnic cullture and, 39–41;
    global, 5, 15, 31, 33, 41, 43, 46; inferiority
    complexes from, 47; modernity and, 1, 2–3,
    4, 6, 11–12, 16, 21, 31, 41–42, 44, 66, 128;
    resistance against, 22, 30; as underside of
    modernity,12, 30, 42, 121–22; zoological, 7
community of sense, 26, 49
Compromise Excluded (Siib video), 76
corpo-politics of knowledge, 128
corruption, 13–14, 18, 21, 90, 131n7
Cow Apa (Suleimenova artwork), 48
creolization, 28, 105, 131–32n2
Crimea, annexation of, 6, 13, 18
crisis of legitimacy, 19, 123

Dagestan, 50–51
decolonial aesthesis, 22–24, 28–31, 35, 36–37,
    39–42; in Caucasus, 49–64; in Central Asia,
    42–49
Defoe, Daniel, 124
defuturing, 12, 120
Deleuze, Gilles, 27
delinking, 23, 24, 28, 29, 31, 32, 41, 51, 119–20,
    132n2
Delinking (Makhacheva artwork), 51
Desert of Oblivion. Quicksand. (Akhunov/
    Borubayeva installation), 103

Dibirov, Magomed, 50
dignity, 31, 32, 46, 124, 126, 128, 133n1
Dilthey, Wilhelm, 28–29
dispensable lives, 7
Doors of the New Tamerlane, The (Akhunov
    painting), 43
Dorzhiev, Zorikto, 47
double-consciousness, 3, 39, 41
Dovlatov, Sergei, 112
Du Bois, W. E. B., 3, 31
Dugin, Alexander, 13, 34
Dussel, Enrique, 132n3
dystopianism, 17, 46

Economist, The (journal), 1
Enlightenment, 15, 121
estate, category of, 7
Estonia, 65, 68, 70, 73–74, 76, 78
ethnic renaissance, 41, 42
Etkind, Alexander, 7
Eurasianism, 91, 132n2. *See also*
    neo-Eurasianism
exoticism, 27, 30, 31, 36, 91, 100–101
exteriority, 125, 132

Fanon, Frantz, 7, 121–22
fascism, 19–20, 34, 36
federalist political model, 37
feminism, 65
Finland, 130n2
Fixation (Pavlensky performance art), 126
Foucault, Michel, 67
Foundling, The (Akhunov), 103
Friction Festival, 52
futurelessness, 16–22, 117, 119, 126. *See also*
    defuturing

Gaisumov, Aslan, 59–64, 126–28
Gamsutl (Makhacheva video), 52
Gattamelata in the Hide of Genghis Khan
    (Meldibekov artwork), 46–47
geopolitics: of being, 69, 128; difference in,
    31; global, 1, 2–3; of knowledge, 29, 128; as
    sacred geography, 132n2; in Ukraine, 53
German, Aleksei, 122
Gioconda Khatun (Dorzhiev painting), 47
globalization, 28, 39, 42, 66
global North, 8–9, 11

global South, 4, 8–9, 121–22
Godard, Jean-Luc, 79, 80–81
Gogol, Nikolai, 35
Gorbachev, Mikhail, 46
Gordon, Lewis, 20–21
Groys, Boris, 9–10, 101
Grozny, Chechnya, 61–62
Guattari, Félix, 27
Guseynov, Orhan, 50

Harris, Wilson, 121
Holy Family (Atabekov assemblage), 45
Household (Gaisumov artwork), 127
human rights, 12, 14, 122

I Am Kazakh (Suleimenova series), 47–48
imperial difference: colonial difference
    and, 3–4, 10, 11–12, 39–42, 65–66, 120,
    129–30n1; decolonizing and, 33, 36, 128;
    effect on Estonia, 65; effect on human lives,
    18; evolution of, 1; external, 2, 10, 14–15,
    119–20, 122, 123–24; internal, 2; modernity
    and, 6, 10
imperial revivalism, 3, 13, 20, 36, 84
inferiority complexes, 10, 16, 47, 129n1
internal colonization, 7, 37, 88, 99
Internal Colonization (Etkind), 7
interstice, 104
irony, 75–77, 80
Islamophobia, 50

Janus-faced empire, 6, 7, 12, 14, 15–16

Kabakov, Ilya, 85
Kadyrov, Ramzan, 61
Kant, Immanuel, 31–32, 68–69, 121
Karimov, Islam, 18
Kazakhstan, 44–49
Kazakov, Yuri, 122
Klyuchevsky, Vassily, 130n2
Kosuth, Joseph, 85
Kristeva, Julia, 72

La Fontaine, Jean de, 78–79
Landscape (Makhacheva art project), 52, 53
language as home, 115–16
Leyenda Negra, La (Black Legend), 14–16
liberating mission, 15

Lionnet, Françoise, 54–55
Lotman, Yuri, 15
Lugones, María, 78

Maffesoli, Michel, 26–29
Magritte, René, 85
Makhacheva, Taus, 45, 50–59
Malevich, Kazimir, 95
Mamedov, Afanassy, 105–18
Marx, Karl, 75
Mass Line: Office 1 (Siib video), 71–72, 77
mass media, 2, 16, 104
Media Impact Festival, 23
Meldibekov, Yerbossyn, 45–46
Member of the Federation (Dibirov painting), 50
memory, 51, 52, 59, 61–62, 69–70, 82, 92, 105,
    113, 119–20, 127–28
metaphysics of the present, 126, 127
Mignolo, Walter, 2, 29
"Mining the Museum" (Wilson installation), 55
Misiano, Viktor, 93, 101
modernity: coloniality and, 1, 2–3, 4, 6, 11–12,
    16, 21, 31, 41–42, 44, 66, 128; hegemony of,
    119; post-Enlightenment, 2, 129n1, 130n2;
    Socialist, 6, 9–10, 19, 24, 91, 94–96, 101,
    102, 130n2; underside of, coloniality as,12,
    30, 42, 121–22
Moraga, Cherríe, 29
Moscow Infantilism, 35
multispatial hermeneutics, 32
Mureşan, Ciprian, 5
"The Museum" (Wilson installation), 55
"A Museum Looks at Itself" (Parrish Art
    Museum), 55

Nargiz and Aramis (Mamedov), 111
National Bolshevism, 13, 34, 36
neocolonialism, 41, 46, 92, 93–94, 100, 124
neo-Eurasianism, 10–11, 34
neoliberalism, 4–5, 18, 22, 27, 39, 42, 66, 70
Nikolayev, Anton, 34, 35–39
No Need for Theories (Gaisumov artwork), 60
non-European former Soviet colonies, 5–6, 7,
    12, 34, 130n2
Non-Standard (Guseynov artwork), 50
nostalgia, Soviet, 5, 38, 71, 73–74, 105
Notarial Office (Suleimenova artwork), 49
nuclear threat, 2

Occupy Abai, 133n1
Occupy movements, 123, 133n1
ontology: aesthesis and, 29; futureless, 119,
    126; human in, 31; relational, 120
Orientalism, 4, 6, 10, 43, 44, 46, 91, 100, 133n1
ornamentalism, 30
Ostojić, Tanja, 5

Paik, Nam June, 103
Pareto, Vilfredo, 26
patriotism, 19
Pavlensky, Pyotr, 23, 125–26
People of No Consequence (Gaisumov photo
    series), 63, 126–27
phenomenological disappearance, use of term,
    122
Piontkovsky, Andrey, 123
Poland, 15, 130n2
postcolonial discourse, 4–5, 11–12
postimperial sensibility, 10, 120
postsocialism, 69–71
postsocialist countries, 4–8, 43. *See also*
    specific countries
post-Soviet condition, 1, 3–4, 8–11
post-Soviet fiction, 108–10
primitivism, 30
progressivism, 4, 6, 8–10, 38, 54, 57
Pushkin, Alexander, 119, 125
Pussy Riot, 23, 125–26
Putin, Vladimir, 12, 17, 123, 131n7

Rabin, Oscar, 85
racism, 5, 10
radical return, 119, 126, 127–28
Rancière, Jacques, 25–26
ratio-centrism, 28–29
re-enchantment, 26, 28
re-existence, 24, 29–32, 124–25, 127, 132n3
refugees, rejection of, 4
repentance, 16, 32, 101–2, 122, 127
resistance, 30–31, 32, 67, 78, 122, 124–26;
    through art, 41–42, 70–71, 80, 83, 120.
    See also re-existence
Return of the Forgotten Regiment (Vereshchagin
    painting), 43–44
road movies, 35, 37
Robbins, Bruce, 32
Rogalev, Egor, *11, 121, 124*

Room of One's Own, A (Siib video-photo
    installation), 72–73
Rossihin, Alexander, 34
ruble, devaluation of, 17
Rushdie, Salman, 78, 114
Russian Federation, 5, 6–7, 8, 13, 50
Russian Orthodoxy, 16, 19–20

Savitsky, Igor, 102
Seam (Pavlensky performance art), 125–26
secessionism, 7, 13
secondary Europeans, 33, 41
secondhand time, 19
Secondhand Time (Alexievich), 9, 19
second-rate empire, 2–3, 12
Security Service (Dibirov painting), 50
self-censorship, 50
self-colonization, 88, 91, 121, 129n1
sense of place, 106
Sentsov, Oleg, 14
Serbia, 15
Serebrennikov, Kirill, 14
Shchapov, Afanasy, 7
Siberia, colonization of, 7
Siib, Liina, 65–83, *66*
silence as resistance, 124–26
Situation No. 2 (Rogalev photograph), *11*
Situation No. 7 (Rogalev photograph), *124*
Situation No. 15 (Rogalev photograph), *121*
slant activism, 75
sobornost, 19
Socialist modernity, 6, 9–10, 19, 24, 91, 94–96,
    101, 102, 130n2
Socialist semi-periphery, 2, 3
solidarity, 31, 32, 65, 75
Solovyev, Vladimir, 14
Son of the East, The (Atabekov assemblage), 44
Sorokin, Vladimir, 14
soup (Dibirov painting), 50
Soviet Union, collapse of, 8. *See also*
    post-Soviet condition
spatial histories, 52, 66, 106
Stalinism, 13–14, 19–20, 131n7
subalternity, 3, 4–5, 33, 43, 65
sublime, 31–32, 47–48
Suleimenova, Saule, 47–49
Super Taus (Makhacheva video), 45, *45*
sweatshop sublime model, 32

Tatlin, Vladimir, 95
Temporary Truce (Dibirov painting), 50
Threat (Pavlensky performance art), 126
Tightrope (Makhacheva video), 57, 57–59
Time of the Tribes, The (Maffesoli), 26
Tolstoy, Leo, 6
transculturation, 105–6, 132n2
transmodernity, 32, 132n3
tribalism, 26–27
tricksterism, 31, 41, 47, 105, 111

Ukraine, 1, 5, 12, 13, 53, 123, 130n2
underside of modernity. *See under* coloniality
unhomed condition, 105–6, 114
unhomeliness, use of term, 66
Union of Soviet Socialist Republics (USSR).
  See Soviet Union, collapse of
Untitled (Gaisumov installation), 62, 62, 64
Untitled (War) (Gaisumov series), 60
USSR Stamps and Seals (Akhunov artwork), 89
utopianism, 16, 18, 19–20, 27, 89, 132n3
Uzbekistan, 18, 42, 84–85, 87, 90–92, 96, 104
Uzbek Transit (Akhunov), 103

Vasnetsov, Victor, 55–56
Vázquez, Rolando, 119
VDNKh (Vystavka Dostizheniy Narodnogo
  Khozyaystva), 57
Vereshchagin, Vassily, 43–44
victory-in-defeat discourse, 16–17, 129n1

Viy (Gogol), 35
Volga (Gaisumov video), 60, 64
Voyna (War), 35

Warrior's Cradle (Atabekov assemblage), 45
Way of an Object, The (Makhacheva artwork),
  55–56, 56
"Weddings" (Mamedov), 116–17
When Everyone Was Kazakhian (Bazargaliev
  series), 47
"White Line" (Bombily performance), 35
white supremacy, 34
Wilson, Frederic, 55
"The Wolf and the Dog" (La Fontaine),
  78–79
woman-space relations, 65–83
Woman Takes Little Space, A (Siib
  photographs), 65, 66, 74, 74–76
Woolf, Virginia, 72–73

xenophobia, 34

Yeltsin, Boris, 17, 46
You Are Following the Correct Road, Comrades
  (Akhunov artwork), 102
Yugoslavia, 13

Zhadan, Serhiy, 14
Zhanaozen (Suleimenova artwork), 49
Zvyagintsev, Andrey, 14

www.ingramcontent.com/pod-product-compliance
Lightning Source LLC
Chambersburg PA
CBHW072141170526
45158CB00004BA/1457